*T*his book is dedicated to those who don't hesitate to step out of their way to help others. To your friends and mine!

However, this is the place for me to express gratitude to Greta Gotlieb, for letting me borrow her laptop in Bali so I could finish this book! Also, to Andrea Scharf for listening whenever I needed an ear. To Sarah Halbeisen for being the most patient human in the universe. And to Annique Senten, for always having my back! Love you!

© 2017 | Monika Kanokova | wearesmartcreatives.com

Editor: **Monika Kanokova**
               hello@mkanokova.com
Copy Editor: **Diana J. Joiner**
               djjoiner925@gmail.com
Illustrator: **Ewelina Dymek**
               ewelinadmk@gmail.com
Art Director: **Christiane Wallner-Haas**
               christiane@wallner-haas.net

A CIP catalogue record for this book is available from the National Library in Austria.

Proudly self-published in Austria in 2017.
ISBN: 978-3-9503967-8-2

Monika Kanokova

An insightful guide for the curious,
the restless, and the adventurous freelancer!

CONTENTS

*H*ello, friend!

I'm so glad you picked up or downloaded this book. It's my third installment and as always, I'm incredibly excited to take you on another inspirational journey. Given you're probably already a freelancer, you might know that freelancing is nothing less than a roller coaster, full of exciting ups and exhilarating downs. Sometimes.

Having called this book *Work Trips and Road Trips*, you might expect to be holding a travel guide for freelancers in your hands on how to be a digital nomad or how to take regular vacations. When I first started researching the content of this guide, this was exactly what I was expecting to write about. But then, while conducting 15 interviews with incredible women whose stories might just blow your mind, I realized there were much deeper subjects that we touched upon.

If you're a newbie to freelancing, you might want to pick up *This Year Will Be Different: An insightful guide to becoming a freelancer* or *My Creative (Side) Business: The insightful guide to turning your side projects into a full-time creative business* before you start reading this book. *Work Trips and Road Trips* is something you'll appreciate once you've set up a business and already have an idea of how you can make money.

If you've read one of my other books, you're probably familiar with the combination of articles and interviews. Conducting these interviews helped me find the right content for the #SMARTCREATIVES guides, and it helped me define the storyline. However, this time around, things are a little different. While you'll still get to read inspiring interviews with women who freelance in the creative industries, I've grouped these interviews and divided the book into five parts.

When I began searching for who I wanted to talk to, I picked women who travel a lot. I figured that if they have so much time and money to be able to afford to hit the road regularly, then there's probably a lot to learn from them. While I learned that money isn't necessarily decisive for how much one can afford to be on the road, your attitude to freelancing and how you see life definitely is!

I hope that #WTART will become a book you'll go back to from time to time, rereading chapters whenever you need a little pick-me-up. You might wonder how to better structure your days, how to take time off for a longer period of time, or when to say "no" if someone presents you with an offer that might sound great, but might not necessarily be the best opportunity for you.

As mentioned above, this book has five parts. In the first section, I'll talk about success and the definition of it. To me, what success means usually correlates with how the society you live in defines it. Then, we'll look closer at mindfulness, which, in my opinion, is a very personal definition of your values, who you are, and who you strive to be. Once we've tackled that, we'll shed some light on what you might already be thinking about when trying to define your purpose. To keep things transparent, another part of this book is dedicated to money, which is also where I'll talk more about time management. Then, to close things off, I've also included a section dedicated to travel.

Now, you might think it all sounds quite spiritual, but given this isn't the first time you've decided to spend some time with my thoughts and observations, you know that I'm too practical and the questions I ask are too detail-oriented for you to dismiss this book before you've dived in.

As always, I'm trying to gather insights into creative freelancing under the hashtag #SMARTCREATIVES. Please use it whenever you want to share a shot of this book, your achievements, your home office, or your vacation on Twitter or Instagram. I can't wait to see what you're up to!

Now, and if you haven't already, make yourself a cup of tea or coffee and enjoy the following pages. You can always let me know you like the book by writing a review on Amazon, or sending me an email to hello@mkanokova.com. Enjoy!

Love,
Monika

*What I am most happy with in life is my
ability to really be in the moment.*

*I'm grateful for my ability to see
the beauty around me.*

*For my capability to acknowledge
that even the bad moments, the moments of doubt,
lead to something good.*

*Knowing that, acknowledging that,
is the gift of the journey called life.*

*It's what made me desire
to publish Work Trips and Road Trips.*

1 ABOUT SUCCESS

*I*n any discussion I'm having, whether it's a societal, personal, or political one, I always come to the conclusion that our intentions are fueled by our egos and how we define success. However, what success means is hardly ever a personal choice. In my opinion, it's what our society - or more specifically, our peers - define as such. Being successful usually demands the comparison to others; having or earning more than them.

Let me ask you this. Whenever you meet someone new, is one of their first questions what you do for a living? And how many times, when replying that you're a freelancer, a solopreneur, did you get a questionable look? Personally, I've gotten quite of a few of these.

From my experience, it's much easier to name the company you work for or drop your job title to get the recognition you most certainly deserve. The more well-known the company is one works for, the more likely is one considered successful.

Capitalism and our meritocracy have set the standard for how we, in the western world, define what it means to be successful. Working, or let's say "keeping busy," makes us feel important. Judging by what the media considers newsworthy, success is often defined by how fast one climbs up the career ladder. It's common for headlines to consist of how much money a startup has raised. Companies are considered more successful with the more employees they have. Status and success are all too often measured in monetary terms, making someone who's constantly busy and in high demand deemed as a more successful human being.

If you're freelancing in the creative industries, chances are high it's even harder for you to say what you do in one word or one sentence. Freelancers tend to start babbling once someone asks them what they do. It's usually a lot to explain and it's not that easy to pin down a definition of how one makes a living. Freelancers will agree the boundaries between work and time off blur, and the question, "What do you do?" might feel intimidating, even after years.

Additionally, the question about someone's job immediately suggests someone puts their work first, which, as you know, isn't always the case. A full-time mom who has a side income as a graphic designer to make ends meet is just as successful to me as a CEO of a large company. Her definition of success is to have time with her kids and their definition is to be in a leadership role and manage people. It's all a question of how one personally defines success.

In 2015, I attended the DNX conference in Berlin, which is a gathering for digital nomads and wannabe remote workers. As a side note, and if you're curious about that sort of lifestyle, I'd recommend going to the next one!

One of the speakers there, Mark Mason, gave an incredibly insightful keynote, and one of the things he talked about that stuck with me was his question, what do you optimize your life for? What is it that you strive for and you believe will lead to a fulfilled life? Is it more money? More time with your family and friends? Independence to travel the world? What is it that you want that will make you feel like you've succeeded at life?

You might've heard that you should never compare yourself to others, but instead, become better than you were yesterday. When coming up with an answer to what would make you feel successful, don't compare yourself to others. Judge by how much time and energy you dedicate to becoming the person you want to be. It's hard to measure things that aren't figurative. Thus, the measurement of your success, if you do need a way to define it, is how close you are in your everyday to the ideal of what you optimize your life for.

If you optimize your life for travel, then it's how you travel that defines your success. If you define yourself by being a good parent, then it's the time you dedicate to playing with your children that makes you successful. If you optimize your life for money, then it's the amount you have in your bank account that gives you proof of how successful you are.

Whether you're a mother (or father) who defines success in terms of providing for your family while also spending time with them, or you're the CEO who feels successful when taking charge of a brand, find your definition of personal fulfillment. Find your optimization and strive for it!

1 THINK ABOUT YOUR LIFE GOALS

I feel like there's no other way to start this chapter than to make you think about quarter life crises. Whether you've had one or not, it's an eligible state of mind in which we question anything and everything we possibly can about life. Around the age of 25 is when we're really faced with setting our future plans. We tempt to feel the pressure of adulthood; we're no longer able to take a raincheck and say we're young and don't know better.

Before we turn 25 (or possibly sooner, maybe a little later), there's always something we work towards that has a framework. We work towards our high school diploma. Then we work towards a college degree. Then maybe a master's degree. Then we need an internship. All of these things are temporary, and what makes them easy – retrospectively, because at the time they all felt really hard – is they come with a set of rules and a goal, which once achieved is clear proof of being successful. However, once you graduate and land your first job, the world with *all* its possibilities is your oyster and you can do whatever you want. The options are limitless, and social media makes opportunities feel equally reachable as it makes them feel out of reach.

Now, and about when a quarter life crisis may kick in, things become quite complicated. Up until now, you knew what rules to play by and what you were trying to accomplish. Once you've gotten your foot into the door of your industry, the regularity of confirmations about how successful you are slows down. Given that many companies have established flat hierarchies, it's difficult to climb higher and prove to ourselves and others what we're worth. It's of no surprise we start questioning what life is all about once we set our own rules and define our own goals. The question suddenly hits us; what are our goals? What is it that's worth working towards forty hours a week, if not more?

Social media makes it seem like everyone has a plan and knows what they're doing and where they're heading. However, once you have an intimate conversation with them, that's not true at all. Not everyone has a clear plan and knows what they want to do with their lives. And even those who do, once they've reached their goals, they'll need to find something new to work towards. Having to constantly define your goals and then redefine them again isn't easy. One doesn't want to set goals that are simple to achieve because then, one would have to quickly find a new one.

So, what is a goal worth having? And what goal do you set yourself, once you've reached one you had? Take becoming a graphic designer or a photographer, for example. What comes after you've added that job position to your LinkedIn or you've built a website that highlights your profession? Now that you're a photographer or a graphic designer, what comes next? We're not made to be satisfied with the status quo. We often seem to want more! But what is it that we want? If we don't have children to take our attention away from ourselves and give us a purpose of helping them achieve their life goals, it's on us to define and redefine the answer to this question for ourselves every day. It's of little surprise millennials want to have an impact. It's the only way we can find assurance that our efforts are needed.

Those who work for a company may have goals set for them and even receive guidance for how to best accomplish these. If, on the other hand, you're a solopreneur, it's in your hands to make plans for what you want to accomplish in the future. There's no one to look after your career. It's you that needs to know what it is you define as personal growth and what makes you feel proud of what you say you do when introducing yourself. Neglecting this sort of self-care is often what leads to the rather common doubts of whether one should look for a proper job again.

Sure, it's uncomfortable to ask yourself the big questions. Why else would you check your emails first thing in the morning instead of diving into the much bigger question of what you want to be doing next right after breakfast? If you don't take the time to be brutally honest with yourself and figure out where you're heading today, tomorrow, in a month, or after a year, you might find yourself at the edge of jumping back into full-time employment. Often, it's the easy way out to have other people tell you what to do instead of finding the answer yourself day after day. Don't get me wrong, working full-time for a company can be a great decision if done for the right reasons. For example, when you find a team that has a mission you can get behind, you respect the team members, you can learn something from them, and you want to be part of that group. Proactively. If you don't find that team or don't want to build it yourself, then keep moving forward, and keep moving forward solo.

Success, especially for freelancers who desire independence, is no longer about climbing the ladder and going up, up, up or growing a team. It's often about going sideways. It's about learning new skills, working with more interesting clients, or increasing the impact that you want to have by working with people who can help you achieve it. It's about creating the sort of work you can be proud of and you believe should exist in this world. Success, in my opinion, is your process. It's your everyday, it's your work-life balance, it's your being in charge of your day. It's the activities you choose to fill up your day with that make you feel content. Activities that make you feel like you're growing as a person and make you feel accomplished.

In my opinion, there are two types of (life) goals; the ones that you can accomplish pretty much yourself by improving your skills, and ones that are accomplished with the help of others. If you focus on making plans that rely on you and your dedication, you might have more luck achieving what you set out to achieve. If, on the other hand, you want to achieve something that depends on others, you might want to balance that goal with a few smaller goals that are dependent solely on you that you can tick off along the way.

2 BE SELF-DETERMINED

———

When you decided to quit your job and go freelance, it might've been because you made more money with your side gig and it just made sense. Or, which is probably more likely, your job didn't allow the freedom you needed. You might've also just had enough of working with the team you were involved in, or got fired from your job and just decided to own it. Whatever the reason was, it set you on the path you're on right now.

(Hi!)

For me, freelancing seemed like the most logical solution to the challenges I was facing in 2014. The life I built for myself fell apart like a house of cards within just a week, and I knew if I wanted to rebuild at least parts of it, I had to find a way to make a living without tying myself to one city. Being able to live location independently usually takes time to build up, and I had no time to take things slow because of the not-so-glorious state of my bank account. The quickest way to transition my workplace into the cloud required me to do something that would show others what I'm capable of. By self-initiating a project, everything else somehow fell into place. As it usually does.

There are two kinds of mentalities; passive and active. A passive mentality allows you to go with the flow and do whatever comes to you without questioning it much. An active mentality is about making conscious decisions and being ready to battle the consequences.

It's about knowing your own values and fearlessly sticking to them.

It's about being bold enough to run your business aligned to your rhythm by your own rules! Success isn't necessarily about living the dream, having a life where everything goes according to plan. It's much more about owning your day, being self-determined, and having the guts to ride the waves, even if you don't have all the solutions necessary to tackle a challenge. There will surely be bad times. Even the people you consider successful have bad days, but you should know that even the worst times are just phases that will pass.

Once you've figured freelancing out, once you've positioned yourself within your field and know how to get clients whenever you run out of assignments (and money), and once you have enough or more than enough work to keep you busy, you will once again probably ask yourself, "Is this it?" or "What's next?".*

Some might have a family and make it the focus of their lives. Others might not be as lucky to have found a partner to start a family with just yet, or might just not feel ready for it or interested altogether. You might also have a family and find yourself at a stage where you have enough "me" time to determine your next career steps, or where you feel you need to make space for yourself.

Generally speaking, for a freelancer, a solopreneur, the incentive for personal growth must come from within. You must be the one to set goals and aims for yourself. It's just a matter of figuring out how to take charge, depending on what stage you're personally at in your life.

For this book, I didn't focus on how to grow your business and how to make more money. (I've already written about those topics in my previous books anyway.) I was far more curious about the stories of people who made freelancing work for them in a way that allowed for more personal freedom. You'll notice that in this book, all of the interviews are travel-related, which might not be as relevant to you because it might not be as desirable to you as it is to others. However, the reason why I conducted all the interviews around travel was because I knew these ladies have thought about self-determination a lot and know how to claim the personal freedom that comes with freelancing.

If you've ever asked yourself whether it's possible to live in a new city every month and learn what it feels to be a local there, I can say, it's possible! Kaitlyn will talk more about it! Do you want to take four to six big trips each year and explore the world at your own pace? Not a problem; Vanessa is living proof that that goal is achievable. You might possibly want to dedicate your life to learning new languages and skills. I had a long conversation with Dani about just that. In a normal job, you'd probably work towards a promotion or look for a new job to feel challenged again. The good news here is that as a free-lancer, you don't even need to quit your job or wait for the opinion of someone else that you're worthy to be promoted. You can promote yourself to have more vacation time, have a four-day work week, sleep in every morning, or work on that big project you've always wanted to do! The time is now!

*If you're not at that point, why not go back to one of my other books, *This Year Will Be Different: An insightful guide to becoming a freelancer* or *My Creative (Side) Business: The insightful guide to turning your side projects into a full-time creative business*, and get some inspiration from what you could do from there?

3 DON'T LET THE DOUBTS CREEP IN

———

Just like any successful creative, there will be times when you'll be faced with doubts. As they say, self-doubt is the worst enemy of creativity (and successful freelancing). As we all know, these thoughts might paralyze you from time to time.

It wouldn't be right to write all this positive pep talk without mentioning that even the most successful creatives have their tough days filled with insecurities. Creativity means navigating new terrain, which is scary and uncomfortable.

If you never had doubts about what you're doing all day long, it would mean you're playing it safe and haven't dared to step out of your comfort zone. Whenever you have a rough day, a rough week, or even a rough month, be easy on yourself. Difficult times usually remind us of the good times, and they're pretty useful when you use them in a constructive way; to rethink what you're doing, what you want to change, and what steps to take to restart. Don't forget, whenever you feel you're not equipped to deal with whatever is making you insecure, try to talk to a friend about it. Or send me an email and I'll make sure to respond and at least try to help!

In times when I feel overwhelmed, I usually lock myself up at home and read books. I either read James Herriot's books because I have a thing for the simple British countryside life. Or, let's be honest, the rather romantic idea of it. But I understand if you don't want to read about a veterinarian from the 1940s that sticks his whole arm into a cow's pelvis. I can also highly recommend Gretchen Rubin's *The Happiness Project* if you need a quick pick-me-up. Even though, hand on heart, James Herriot's writing is pretty damn hilarious!

Once you're done moping because you're not someone whose creativity is fueled by struggle, it might not be that easy to get back to work. Nevertheless, the only way to overcome what's bothering you is by facing it, just from a different perspective. Try a new technique that you've never tried before, look for a collaborator, and whenever doubt hits you, always remember that Walt Disney was fired from the *Kansas City Star* in 1919 because his editor said he "lacked imagination and had no good ideas." It's normal to have doubts, but don't let them overwhelm you!

4 SELF-INITIATE PROJECTS

———

In good economic times, if you've done great work and if the word about your services have spread, chances are high many new requests for your business have come from referrals. The longer you've been in business and the more you've established yourself as a reliable person that delivers high quality work, sooner or later, there will be enough work coming to keep yourself busy and enough money to have a good life. If you ask for it.

In *My Creative (Side) Business*, I talked a lot about creative entrepreneurship, how you should think about your skills, and how to best turn them into products that you can then sell. Freelancers tempt to take on work as it comes. If they're out and looking for work, they often take whatever falls into their lap first to pay the bills. While at times this is reasonable, over a longer period of time, it can become quite exhausting. Because people might want things from you that you might not be all too keen to do. From my experience, the most effective way to make others aware of what you're good at is by making what you enjoy doing tangible. When I decided to write *This Year Will Be Different*, I was working on a six-week long project full-time. I didn't need to do something extra to keep myself busy. I was busy. Instead, I needed to feel like I was working on something that was truly meaningful to me. I was craving to work on a project that would connect me with people I wanted to connect with. On one hand, I wrote the guide because it was a good exercise in long-form writing and I knew I'd learn something new. On the other hand, which I didn't know at the time, it made people aware of my skills and interests who then approached me with potential assignments. Just the fact that I got

Kickstarter as a client after having done a Kickstarter project myself and spent the next two years working with them truly is the proof of what's possible.

When I talk about self-initiated projects, I don't necessarily talk about finding yourself a hobby. Self-initiated projects can still make you money. Maybe not today, maybe not tomorrow, but your aim should be that your time investment pays off eventually.

If you have enough work coming your way, you might think I'm crazy to suggest you should self-initiate projects at all. If you're temporarily overwhelmed with contract work, you might also wonder why you should carve out time for personal projects with your already busy schedule. It's mostly because self-initiated projects (or raising your hand when you hear someone's looking for help in a field you want to get into) help steer your business into the direction you want to go. Discovering and following through with projects will help you access the people you want to access, acquire new skills, and you'll have something to talk about, which will help you feel much more accomplished and thus, successful. Even in times that might be hard for you! Having that feeling of accomplishment might serve as a bridge to better times and give you new energy for another project!

When coming up with a project, don't forget that it always has to have a clear outcome. There's a difference between an initiative and a project. If you start a series of events – just to give you an example – then, in the long-term, you add something to your workload that will eventually become just another task on your to-do list. So make sure that when you say you're working on a project, it really is a project and it has a clear outcome and a deadline. Even if it's a flexible one. With projects, in contrast to initiatives, you know when they're over and when it's time for you to celebrate!

5 CELEBRATE! AND CELEBRATE OFTEN

When was the last time you had a glass of champagne for breakfast to celebrate your latest success? I'm not saying you should develop bad habits. You might prefer an extra-incredible smoothie instead, however, you should acknowledge the moment of accomplishment and raise a glass to yourself! Cheers!

Once you've finished an assignment or accomplished a project, before you move onto the next task, take a moment for yourself and celebrate! Go out for a fancy breakfast, or take a day or a week off. Do whatever gives you the space to be proud of yourself. After all, given you're a freelancer and very likely working by yourself most of the time, there's no one to put a piece of an extra fancy cake on your table to cherish this little, big moment!

If you're someone who tempts to overlook what's worth celebrating, but always keeps moving, google Tim Ferriss' "The Jar of Awesome." That might give you some guidance on how to look out for the small wins, or in other words, the moments of success. Freelancing can be lonely at times, so having a friend who's also a freelancer to celebrate with makes life much better! If you don't have anyone who's chosen a similar career path, a path of independence, try to find someone online to celebrate with. I'm currently working on a solution to help #SMARTCREATIVES connect with each other, so if you haven't heard of it yet, please shoot me an email to hello@mkanokova.com so I can let you know what's the latest! Also, I can always make sure to raise a glass to your success over Skype or comment on Instagram if you tag the image with #SMARTCREATIVES. Yay! (Yay! Again!)

When choosing what interviews I'd assign to each section of this book, I immediately thought of Dani Bradford, Vanessa Bruckner, and Theresa Lachner for the first part; the chapter about success.

I met Dani Bradford at Ryan Holiday's masterclass at the 99U conference in New York. She was sitting next to me and we started chatting while waiting for the talk to start. She mentioned she used to work as a designer for *National Geographic*, but that most of the time she travels the world. She vagabonds. She didn't care for big names or what others thought of her. She cared about her experiences and making life a daring journey. It stuck with me!

It's the same attitude I highly admire about Vanessa, an Austrian journalist. She seems so self-confident about her skills and she knows what she brings to the table. She trusts herself and she knows that even the worst days can be turned into great stories, thus becoming her capital, not her burdens. If that isn't success, I don't know what is!

Theresa, a German sex blogger, never cared about what's appropriate to say or not say. She writes whatever she thinks. Her honesty and clarity and her ability to put herself out there worry-free of other people's judgements is highly admirable. Her authenticity is striking, and so is her story!

I hope you get some valuable takeaways and gain some more confidence from reading the following three stories!

DANI
BRADFORD

MAKE LIFE
A DARING
ADVENTURE!

What's been your educational and professional path?
At first, I studied Fine Arts, but then I realized how important it was to learn how to promote myself. I wanted to have a degree that was more business-oriented, so I switched majors to Graphic Design. It was a practical decision; I always pictured myself as an artist, but I knew how important it was to learn more about the commercial side of professional life. I'm really glad I made that decision because I love the path my life has taken me.

During my studies, multimedia sounded particularly interesting, so even though I was studying graphic design, I signed up for a video class. When I graduated, I started working as a videographer for a non-profit organization. Part of my job was to travel to developing countries to set up conferences, shooting b-roll and photos in the field. I learned a lot about food security, poverty, nutrition, and women's rights. Getting involved with these issues inspired me to start a blog and work on personal projects to tell stories I believed mattered – I've been documenting these stories and photos on http://lonerucksack.com.

As a creative, there's rarely just one thing that you do. Part of being a creative freelancer is that you're creative about how you make a living. It's essential to build different income streams. My entire career, now that I reflect on it, has been built on finding something I enjoyed doing and pursuing it. It has brought me clients, such as *National Geographic, USA Today,* and Under Armour. I started freelancing with Under Armour after I got back from backpacking around Africa, and did a project with *National Geographic* after flying back to the states from cycling across Europe. I often find that many people are afraid to try to make a living doing something they enjoy. However, it's worked for me, so why shouldn't it work out for others?

When you study design, you often think you'll end up working at some swanky agency in a city like London or New York. But I can say, there are other and far more exciting opportunities available to you as a creative professional, especially if you're not driven by money. I think it's important to be passionate about what you do. For me, I have a drive for storytelling and photography and I want to write about the people I meet. I'd say my goal in life is to think about what I'm learning and how I can use that acquired knowledge and contribute to this world in a positive way. There's so much to see and learn, and I'd love to help people see what's happening in parts of the world they might not be aware of.

How is your business set up?

I'm a freelance art director. I design, I photograph, I tell stories. Okay, call me a digital storyteller! I design websites for clients, create logos, and I art direct social media accounts or even shoot products if my clients need photos that reflect my kind of lifestyle. I do a lot of different things.

Since I left my full-time job as a videographer, I've found balance by working for a year or two and then taking a year off. I feel very strongly about living the lifestyle I do. Being a female that travels solo seemed unattainable to women just a few years ago, so I really want to show girls and women that living as independently as I do is possible. With my blog *Lone Rucksack*, I've created a brand centered around being an adventurous outdoor woman. I guess that's also why some brands like working with me and why they hire me to work on their visual identities. Being at the art director level, I earn more than what I need. I try to be mindful of my spendings during the times I work full-time to make my money last longer. Then, when I'm traveling full-time when it's my year off, I'm actually not off at all. I still work. I just work with the mindset that I'm not trying to make a full-time living, but rather spend time on personal projects that are important to me. Those also help me keep updated on what's happening in the design world, which is crucial when I want to keep working at the art director level. In the past couple of months, I've become more focused on trying to make money with my side projects. So that's the next step!

When I look back at the past seven years, I love what I've accomplished: there's no difference between a career and a life. Whether it's learning to surf, learning a new language, or working on a project for an amazing company like National Geographic, those things are all part of my career and my lifestyle. The mind of a creative never stops. I'm not someone who likes to look in the air and do nothing. I really like creating things. I'm fascinated by the people and places I surround myself with and I love to tell their stories.

It's strange to me that a lot of people think I don't work just because I don't sit in a physical office. Yes, I don't work for another company and I don't let earning money take over my life, but I still "do" things. I get up early, I go to bed super late, and I create throughout the day. So I am working, just not for someone else and not at a physical office space.

How would you describe your attitude towards travel?
I'd call myself a dirtbag adventure traveler. I travel solo and I'm very vocal about being a female traveler who goes to places off the beaten path. One of the reasons I write my blog and am active on social media is that I'd like to be a role model for young women. I think that's an important thing to be because when I was growing up, there weren't many strong females to look up to in the media. It's important to be conscious of this. I'm now over thirty and I'd consider myself a very experienced traveler, yet I still have people say the most ridiculous things about what I shouldn't be doing because I'm a female. It's all these imaginary dangers people

picked up from the media and then think are going to happen to me because I'm a solo female traveler.

When I travel, I don't need much; really just the minimum. A sink and a hot plate will do. In 2015, I went on a cycling trip and only had a shower every seven days and it was all fine. To me, sleeping in a bed and having a mosquito net is really exciting. It's all I need. The places I go fuel my curiosity and give me stories to tell.

It's not that I woke up one day while still living in the house I owned and thought to myself, "I'll go biking for several months and only have one shower per week." It's definitely been a progression. I used to have a boyfriend, a house, a car, and a regular lifestyle, but I increasingly felt unhappy. One day, I was at a conference in Jakarta. I had the best time! I loved the culture. I loved meeting all the people. I loved editing all the videos, even though I didn't sleep much during that time. I simply loved everything about the experience and I thought to myself that my life could be like that all the time. I then spontaneously booked a flight to Bali. I wasn't far away, so why not? Then, sitting in Bali and drinking a beer at the beach all by myself, it was such a revelation. A turning point, really. I realized I could do whatever I wanted. At that time, I wasn't happy about renovating the house or about how my relationship was going. I returned home, broke up with my partner, sold the house, I moved some of my personal things and my personal documents to a storage space in Baltimore, and I started traveling. I don't think you go from having a house in the city to traveling, knowing you won't have a shower for seven days, from one day to another. Only now, I know it's not a big deal. It's been a progression.

How did you start implementing travel into your work life? How did you set up the business side of things?
I worked for a company that set up and also paid for all my travels. They even took care of all my visas! I don't think I would've started cold turkey, just traveling the world by myself. Before that job, I had only been on a couple of trips with friends; going to Mexico for

two weeks or so, just really the kind of trips you take when you have a regular lifestyle. But after that job, it felt natural to go to all these places by myself.

Once I quit my job, I changed my lifestyle radically. I'd work in the US at a company for a limited period of time to earn money before taking off again. I've optimized my life for new experiences.

Given I have no home address, I've set up my business in the cloud. I have a Traveling Mailbox, which functions essentially like an email inbox, but just for tangible mail. I have a P.O. box in Florida, even though I've never lived there. It's where I forward all my mail and checks. When I work with clients, I usually require a 50% deposit and it's great to know these go directly to my P.O. box. It's a great service because they scan all my mail and upload it, which gives me access wherever I am in the world.

At the beginning before I started traveling, I was a customer at a particular bank, but they always charged me incredibly high international fees, so I switched to PNC bank. There are all sorts of bits and pieces you should look into before you hit the road.

How do you, at your level, communicate to your clients you're only going to work there for a limited period of time before taking off again? How do you make sure they don't forget about you?
I've never actually done that. Really. It's not that I arrange to go back to the US for three months to then take off again. I don't like to plan like that. It's more that if I come across an opportunity I'm excited about, I'd apply and move back. Then, anything could happen!

I once worked for *National Geographic* for a project. Originally, I was only supposed to be there for three weeks, but then it worked out so well that I stayed much longer. It's not that I'd plan out my next two years. I do things and they usually lead to something else that I think is a great opportunity. I believe that if you would go in thinking you'll only stay for six months, you might close yourself off to further opportunities. But whenever I leave, I always try to maintain continuous professional relationships, which isn't easy when you're on the road. Especially when you're in the moment, your clients and the professional world often feels very far away. That's something that's not just challenging with professional relationships. It's the same for personal ones too! I travel solo, so keeping up with people is difficult. I feel like I'm always leaving people and don't get to know them very well. There's something really special about knowing someone for five or ten years. I really love having people around me who are dear to me that I can spend unconventional, intimate time with. I don't have those moments often. Of course, others might feel a little jealous when they see how my life is, but then, really the pasture often seems greener on the other side.

Continuous relationships with people is something I think about a lot. When you're in a stable environment, an office environment for example, you get to talk to people regularly because they're just there, but once you're out of that environment, you must make an effort to keep in touch and regularly let people know you're available for projects. What's also challenging is that a lot changes in the design field, so it's not just about maintaining your professional relationships with people, but you must also keep an eye on the latest trends to stay updated. You need to know what's going on in the ecommerce field, or what sort of websites are popular these days.

Social media has made it easier to keep in touch with what other professionals in your field are doing, and to also keep in touch with them. I read a lot of blog posts or tech publications to stay on top of what's happening in the UX and UI field.

Being a full-time traveler, how do you maintain relationships?
That's probably the biggest challenge and a trade off of a location independent life. Given I've optimized my life for experiences, meeting people has become one too, just usually short-term. I really always hope I'll run into people again. I guess no one can have

it all. On the other side, every single day is just so exciting. I learn something every day. Just walking down the dirt street with my notebooks, heading to a Spanish class gives me such a thrill. It's a gift to feel like the day mattered because of something new I've learned.

How does it work out financially for you?

I spend very little. I'm very conscious of every buying decision I make. I always think to myself, "Is this something I really need?" In my opinion, a lot of people spend a lot of money on things I don't think are necessary, but other people don't even think about it. Is a $4 cup of coffee really necessary? Do you really need it? No, you don't. It's a luxury. I like to keep a frugal budget and save the majority of my earnings.

When I was living in DC working for *National Geographic*, I moved into a ridiculously cheap room in a group house with people from all over the world. Our basement was filled with bikes because we all cycled to work. I had the tiniest room and I'd bike three miles to work every day. I like that sort of minimalist lifestyle. I'm okay not having a car. I like taking public transport. I like biking. But I also know it's easy to get wrapped up in a lifestyle that costs much more. Sometimes, it's easy to go with what you think you should want rather than thinking about what you should have. I think it's a distinction. Many times, people make these distinctions based on societal influence rather than thinking critically about what they want.

Of course, it's nice to go out with your colleagues to some swanky place and order a soy milk cappuccino and enjoy it. It's fun to do these things, but then you have to choose what really is your top priority. For me, my lifestyle as it is is a priority, which means that the $4 coffee cannot be if I want to sustain how I'm living my life. When you have the sort of lifestyle where a $4 cup of coffee is the norm, it's hard to say no. It feels awkward at first, but I realized you'll eventually get over it. When your colleagues want to go to a happy hour, you can still join and just order a water or a soft drink instead of spending $20 on cocktails just to fit in. You can be part of those activities, just without spending as much. I know I can keep my expenses very low. When I'm in the US, I save up, but when I'm traveling, I don't get a regular paycheck each month, so I spend more and don't earn as much besides the income from my blog.

My ideal of how much I would like to make each month is what I used to make when I was fully employed. But I also know it's not my highest priority. As long as I can save money from what I earn, it's all good. When I was younger, I wasn't as careful as I am now, but I like to keep a cushion. There were times I didn't have that, which I think is also good. It's good to have an empty bank account from time to time. It's an experience and it helps build character. However, I'm very aware that even saying that is very privileged. In the US, it's normal for people not to have more than $2,000 in their bank account at any given time. Many live from paycheck to paycheck. As a freelancer, you can always set your priorities in such a way that you dedicate more hours to work and thus earn more. I've definitely had times where I was running low on funds and needed to send out my resume to a lot of companies and get in touch with professional contacts for work to ramp up my bank account.

How do you budget for your travels?
When I first started traveling, I had money because of what I got from selling the house my ex-partner and I renovated over three years. It was an asset. But now, I don't want to have assets. I don't want a house or a car. I want to have experiences.

When I left for my cycling trip through Europe for six months, I had $10,000 saved. I was almost out of money at the end of the trip, but it was fine because I knew I could earn it again. In many places, you might just need about $10 per day to get around.

What's something you'd recommend to others who want to travel the way you do?

Be open and humble. Be open to new experiences and new people and dare to say "yes," even if it scares you. Even if you're not sure, do it anyway. You'll at least learn something. Traveling sucks sometimes. It's hard. So be very aware of why each day is important, then each week will be important, then each month, then each year, and eventually, you'll look back and be living the life you wanted because each day meant something.

Dani Bradford on
Web: lonerucksack.com
Instagram: @lonerucksack

VANESSA BRUCKNER

DON'T WORRY ABOUT WHERE YOU'RE GOING, JUST KEEP IT INTERESTING!

What's been your educational and professional path?
I had a very supportive teacher in German class when I was in school and he said I was never going to become a Goethe, but I'd be good enough to measure up to Schiller if I kept working on my craft. Writing's always been something I've been good at and very confident about, and that's why I studied Communications and Publishing, and also Arts History.

I've always done a lot of internships, and to support myself, I took on about any job offered to me, from babysitting to selling jewelry. I've never felt I was better than any sort of job I was offered, and I guess because I was easy and pleasant to work with, more opportunities came my way. By the time I graduated, not only had I already built a great professional network; I also had enough work experience under my belt for me to get a regular job with a contract. Something unheard of in my branch.

I worked for a national TV station doing the daily news. Even though it sounds exciting, the reality is that every day is the same. That really wasn't for me! Subconsciously, I knew I had to change something! Then, someone recommended the movie *Eight Miles High*, which is about the life of Uschi Obermaier. She was such a free spirit and I immediately felt inspired! Don't ask me why, but at 2 am, I had an urge to quit my job and I did. I sent an email to my boss announcing my termination. It's not that I had a plan. I didn't. But I knew I was ready for an adventure! I thought I'd like to do something with photography. I applied as an assistant to two photographers in Germany and the one in Hamburg invited me to come in to introduce myself. When things are supposed to work, they always do, and I got a job offer on the spot! When I walked out of the appointment, I spotted a note on an advertising column: someone was looking for a tenant. I called them up and they invited me to come immediately. I got the apartment and within an hour, I had a job and a place to stay!

A month later, I was living in Hamburg with everything I owned. Since then, I've learned that if you think about something for a while that you consider risky, you should just simply do it! It will work out! Because you can make it work out!

That attitude led me to take the next step in my career. In 2013, I decided to go freelance and write for different magazines. I mostly focus on human interest stories and I often write about travel. Additionally, I write commercial copy and press releases for brands.

How is your business set up?

I'm a freelance journalist and a copywriter. I work for various women's magazines and for a local TV station. Besides writing, I've also slowly established myself as a creative copywriter for brands. I produce concepts for commercials and print ads, and I also come up with brand slogans.

I worked for the magazines before I started freelancing for them, so I'm usually invited to the editorial meetings. I always make sure to never come unprepared! Editorial meetings are where I secure my assignments for the following months. I bring at least ten ideas for stories to every single meeting I'm a part of. They're stories I deeply care about, stories I really want to write. I know that being so invested in a coverage makes it easier for me to convince others why it's a good idea to run it as an article. Of course, I can't write the tenth story about a day trip in Stockholm, but I can always look for new angles and perspectives.

I'd really say that writing is the smallest part of a journalist's job. It's research and the ability to spot stories where others might not see them, then to tell these stories in a compelling way for others to care. There are billions of people and at least as many stories. I don't think I'll ever run out of stories to tell. I'll just have to find different ways to tell them.

When I was in Stockholm, for example, I walked up to several women and asked them to spend 30 minutes with me to show me *their* Stockholm. I wanted to see and experience the city from their personal angles. It wasn't just a great way to see Stockholm through their eyes, but I also learned a lot about their personal lives. This is the thinking I'm talking about. Coming up with these sort of concepts is the hard work. Not the writing.

I guess the essence of how I work is that I know many people. Online research isn't where you find the most interesting stories because those are stories someone else has already told.

How would you describe your attitude towards travel?
I'd call myself a flashpacker. I used to backpack, but now I'm in my mid-thirties and I like to keep a certain standard. I no longer want to sleep in a dorm room with ten other people because I like my sleep too much. Once you have an income, you no longer need to do everything on the cheap. If there's a trip I really want to take, I no longer think about the finances. I just do it.

Simultaneously, it's really important to me to have a home. I love bringing souvenirs back from my travels and decorate my apartment with things I fell in love with somewhere on the road. I pack too much already; too many cosmetics, and too many clothes (I really can't decide what I'll need once I'm out there). But then, I know it's me who has to carry around that suitcase. I've learned to accept it. It's simply how I am!

I've always traveled, and mostly on my own. It helps me better understand myself. You also meet more people than if you were to travel with someone. It's a very different experience to sit on the other side of the world with someone you know because it still feels familiar and comfortable. If you're by yourself and if you're a social person, you won't be alone for too long and you'll feel much more connected to your surroundings.

How did you start implementing travel into your work life after you went freelance?

When I travel, I always bring a notebook and my camera. Wherever I am, I'm looking for stories. I know that I'll only be able to focus on my environment if I'm not distracted. As a journalist, I sell these stories, so while travel fills me up, it's also how I make a living. I write about my experiences and then once I get back home, I offer the stories to magazines and usually I always find a publisher for all of them. My rule is that wherever I go, I'll have to find a way to monetize a trip so it pays for the flight and the accommodation afterwards, either with selling one story, or sometimes two!

How do you communicate to your clients you're not going to be available?

Working and traveling requires being organized. You need to keep everyone in the loop and keep your deadlines in check. You need to tell people when you're going to be gone and when they should expect to receive your work. If you're going away for longer, you also need to sublet your apartment to someone reliable, so that's an additional layer of bureaucracy. But I really think whoever works in the creative industries will master administration sooner or later and if not, one can always get an agent.

I collect stories whenever I travel, and that's also what my clients hire me for. However, given I write a lot of human interest stories and these are often local, I make sure to deliver before I take off on one of my adventures. With five magazines I write for regularly, I contribute between one and two stories to each one a month. Then, copywriting and concepting is something I can take with me on the road. It's not that I won't be available; I'm still very responsive. Work to me doesn't feel like something I don't enjoy. I'm more than happy to reply to emails and be there for people.

Being self-employed, how do you balance your work life?

In some ways, I always work. I like going to events a lot, so even when I don't work in the most traditional way, I'm still doing something that benefits my career. Of course, it's not all fun and games like in the Uschi Obermaier movie or on all the countless blogs that show you happy people with their laptops on a beach. It often sounds more romantic than it actually is. Sometimes a magazine sends me somewhere to write, but usually my travels are self-initiated. I travel for at least three months each year. I don't like Europe in the winter, or cold weather really.

I travel partly for work, partly for leisure. However, I love to walk around with my camera and take pictures, which you might call leisure, but given I sell these photos along with my stories, it's also work. Work and travel is one and the same for me. That's what I really love about it!

I'm not someone who has a routine. I don't plan to get up every day and write from 9 am until 12 pm, wherever I am on this planet. When I don't have a deadline, I only write when I feel inspired or when I think I'll forget the details that I believe are important if I don't write it down immediately. Only writing when I feel inspired is also why I get it done much faster. I usually carry around pen and paper, so I always jot down notes. It's not that if I'm traveling, I'm partying all the time. Sometimes I spend the night editing, other times writing, and then I might go out from time to time.

It's really important for me to do the things I do very consciously; to take pictures very consciously, to write very consciously. I'm not someone who runs around with a smartphone, capturing everything I see to post it on my Instagram. I'm really aware of the moments when I take photographs. I know that when I take a picture of something, I simultaneously lose the moment, which I decided to photograph instead. For that reason, I also don't use Instagram. I don't want to lose myself in other people's heads to think about what they think about me. I'd much rather experience the moment as it is. Without a filter.

As you might have noticed, I don't like doing things half-heartedly. I can't write when there's something that bugs me. That's why I don't like to do things last minute. Of course, I might have times where I lock myself up to finish articles that I promised to deliver, but usually I keep buffers. When I travel, I don't bring the sort of work with me where I must respect any sorts of deadlines. I want to have the freedom to only write when I feel like it and to be fully present and immersed in the local culture. But, then again, not wanting to do things half-heartedly also means I want to be conscious of what I do. I want to be conscious of the times I work and conscious of when I relax and then really embrace it. La Dolce Vita, the Italian way of life, feels really close to who I am.

Growing up in Austria, you learn to work really hard. Work is our culture's focus. But in Italy, they'll get a glass of wine and strike up philosophical conversations about how good the wine tastes. I love that!

How does it work out financially for you?
I have several editors that I work for regularly. In my mid-thirties, I know what sort of content works for what publication, so I pitch to the editors accordingly. With some magazines, I participate in the editorial meetings and I always make sure to have at least ten ideas that I can suggest. There will always be at least one story they really like and ask me to write. Then, I also sell the stories I write during my travels.

Of course, it hasn't worked like that since I first decided to be a journalist. It's taken two and a half years until I was able to live off of my freelance income, and I really worked my butt off to get there. Additionally to my profession as a journalist, I picked up copywriting and creating concepts for commercials because that usually brings much more money.

I have a safety cushion of around €5,000 that I have saved up and try to keep at that level. I add about €300 monthly, even though this is also the fund I use when I book flights.

How do you budget for your travels?

I spend my savings on travel. I'm not someone who gets a manicure every other week or buys a new handbag. Whatever I earn, I spend on what's most important to me: seeing the world.

I usually book my flights way in advance, and I book an accommodation for the first two or three nights and then look for one once I get to my destination. Sometimes, I don't pay to stay somewhere. Instead, I trade my skills: I offer to take pictures of the accommodation or write texts for a company's website. I'm very open minded and generally interested in people. It hardly ever takes long for me to meet the chef or owner of a restaurant. I have the gift to see possibilities where others don't, so it's relatively easy for me to convince others about my ideas. Pointing out possibilities and opportunities to people and then offering them help with execution, you quickly make people curious about what else you could do for them.

It's not easy to budget because my spendings depend on the destination. There are some places where you can live like a king and others where a €1,000 spending budget doesn't bring you as far. I plan my travels throughout the year and I also think about where I want to go each year. I can't just go to San Francisco, Australia, or Britain all the time because then I could only go somewhere twice a year for a few days. I try to explore places where it's easier for me financially.

What's something you'd recommend to others who want to travel the way you do?

Make an effort to keep in touch with the people you meet. If someone touches your heart, you shouldn't let them go so easily, and there are tools that help you participate in other people's lives even when they live in another city. For example, I met someone in Munich, who then saw I was heading to Sri Lanka. They decided to join and then one other friend came with us too. Then, with someone else who I had met in Australia, we always said that when they go to Rome, I'd join them, so when I got an email saying they were attending a conference, I immediately booked my flight. At another point, I also gave the key to my apartment to someone I met on a train because they were let down by someone on Couchsurfing. I didn't need my apartment for a few days, so why not have someone else stay there? Sure, it might be travel that makes you be open to people, but I guess being open and approachable to people is also what can make life far more fulfilling.

David Bowie said, "I don't know where I'm going, but I promise it won't be boring." That's pretty much my life's motto. It's fun!

Vanessa Bruckner on
Web: pfirsichblau.com

THERESA LACHNER

DISCONNECT
TO RECONNECT

What's been your educational and professional path?

I studied Comparative European Literature, Publishing, and Communications. My plan was to do something with media. Anything, really. However, after a year, I got bored of studying media and decided to take on another major to focus on literature. I really just wanted to read books and travel, and here and there I'd do an internship.

Even before I graduated, I would travel. First, I went around Italy, then to Amsterdam, then to Berlin, all before going to Asia. It's not that I would've taken off to travel; I was still working. I just didn't want to study and write my thesis at the library. I took my work with me. I knew I could finish a book exposé and also my master's thesis in Bangkok, Chiang Mai, and Bali, so that's what I did!

Then, I went back to take my oral exams. Ironically enough, on my way back to school, I received an email from a publisher I had applied to work for. The job was in Vietnam and they said they'd love to have me! Knowing what I'd do after university really took off the pressure. I graduated, I went to catch the plane, and I left!

Once I got to Saigon, I realized the job was nothing like what I expected. It really was just basic research work: I was hired to correct captions on images. It was the sort of thing where if the caption said a painting was at the Louvre, I'd have to make sure it really was at the Louvre and not at the Eremitage or somewhere else. It wasn't even that I really wanted to move to Saigon in the first place, I just wanted to live somewhere outside of Europe. I knew nothing about Vietnam before I moved there; I just knew I liked noodle soup. Frankly, I thought that was good enough for me to just risk it! And that's pretty much how my life as a digital nomad started!

How is your business set up?
I write about sex and sometimes travel. But really, mostly sex. Sex is something not a lot of people want to write about openly or under their real name, so I've found a niche for myself. I first started writing about sex when I was 22. Once people picked up on my writing style, I got more and more offers. My approach to writing is that I try things so you don't have to. If I write about bondage, then I've been tied up myself. If I didn't like it, I'll write why I didn't like it. If I decide not to have sex for a while, I write about why I don't have sex. I think what qualifies me as a sex writer is that I explore the topic from every single angle there is. I've even written my thesis about feminism, so I cover that angle too!

Working at an office has never really worked out for me. When you work for magazines, what you can actually write about is very limited. You can't explore topics like homosexuality or sex parties as openly because advertisers don't really want their ads next to those articles. The way magazines are curated, there's just a lot of marketing involved. Every headline gets tested and every piece is considered around how suitable it is to pair with ads. It's business!

The first article I wrote about sex was quite odd. I got into the office where I interned and they handed me some notes about a vibrator someone's dad wrote. I was supposed to turn those notes into an article. It was really, really odd! But then, once I lost the mental barrier and accepted that sex was just another topic and one that's relevant to all of us, it became normal and actually very exciting! Sex is something everyone relates to in one way or another. I like talking to people about what I do because being frank and honest about sex often leads to interesting conversations.

In 2015, I started publishing my writing on a blog. I bumped into a guy from Germany, Tim Chimoy, and he suggested I should start a blog. As a journalist, at first I didn't understand why I should give away content for free if I could get paid for it, but Tim was so nice to explain how much he earned with his ebooks and affiliate sales. He was very transparent about how his business worked and it sounded fascinating! I knew I needed to find joy in writing again, and I gave it a shot. Having a blog didn't just help me love writing again, it really changed the game for me! It gave me freedom!

I don't write about sex the way society wants us to think and feel about it. I don't write about sex to please advertisers. I write about the things I think and feel are important. I really try to capture intimacy in words. My first article was about a feminist-friendly porn movie. We've all seen the regular stuff. I felt it was enough!

On my blog, I can choose what gets published. And very quickly, it turned out, there were enough people who wanted to read what I wanted to write. The blog became popular. Now, it's what I do full-time! Or let's say, not full-time, it's just what pays all my bills. Thanks to my minimalist lifestyle, I don't have to earn as much.

As a blogger, parts of my income are generated by my reach and not just through my journalistic work. I help others with their social media strategy too, which pays better than writing and it allows me to only do the sort of journalistic work that I enjoy. I write between two and five articles a month.

Thanks to my blog, I'm a writer and a speaker, and publishers are also approaching me with book deals. Life really gets easier if you can be found on the internet! I still contribute to magazines; *Business Punk*, *Cosmopolitan*, *Jolie*, and *Spiegel Online* are some that book me as a writer. I have sponsors on my blog and I do some copywriting for corporates in Germany.

How would you describe your attitude towards travel?
I've only come across the term "digital nomad" in 2015. I was looking for a suitable health insurance and that was a term that sounded like me: a remote worker who conducts their life in a nomadic manner.

Everywhere I go, I work, just like people who live in one country. Similar to having a normal office job, I take two trips a year where I disconnect and don't even pack my laptop. Over time, my attitude to how often I go somewhere new has changed. I used to have an itinerary and have the months ahead planned out. I'd know where I'd be the next week. Now, when I like a place, I stay longer. I've realized with the freedom I've created for myself, I should be free enough to live by the day.

Booking flights, when you're flexible with the dates, can become extremely affordable. Whenever I look for flights, I check for the entire month and look at the various options. When I see cheap flights on Skyscanner, months and months ahead, I'll usually just book them. For example, I found a flight from Pisa to Brussels for €17 including tax. I knew I needed to be in Brussels around that time, so I booked it. Even if I wouldn't have ended up taking the flight, it was still only €17. I'd survive that! It helps being flexible. Additionally, I know how much flights cost. Roughly. I know that when I book a flight from Europe to Asia, it should cost around €600 or €700 for an open jaw return trip. If it's more, I'm not going to book.

What's changed for me over the last few years is I value my time and freedom more than money. I allow myself to change my mind. Sometimes, that might cost me €200, but because my time and my freedom matter more to me, I know it's just €200. As a freelancer, €200 is less than a half-day remuneration. How you look at money strictly depends on your personal priorities.

How did you start implementing travel into your work life after you went freelance?
The publisher in Saigon had a deal that if you stayed for three months, they paid for your flights. When I left, I decided to continue traveling. I was already freelancing for the German *Cosmopolitan*, and their pay for one article was more than what I earned at the publisher in a month. It didn't take much money to feel rich!

There was another job I applied for before I took on the job with the publisher in Vietnam for a Swiss travel guide publisher, *JPM Guides*. I told them openly that I didn't plan on moving back to Europe anytime soon, but offered to help with their Asian guides. When you think of how you can contribute to companies, you might end up finding a compromise that will work as much to your advantage as it will work to your client's advantage. They ended up hiring me and I corrected and wrote the travel guides for Myanmar, Singapore, Thailand, Vietnam, and Laos. It wasn't a great salary if I lived in Switzerland, but it was more than enough to have a marvellous life in Asia!

I've always known that wherever I go, I want to live my life, travel, and work in a way that's meaningful to me, where I have the sort of life experience that fulfills me. Travel does just that, which is why it's such a core part of how I live my life.

How do you communicate to your clients you're not going to be available?

I have a strong voice as a writer and when you read my articles, you know how I tick. That makes it easier because the sort of clients who hire me want exactly that. They want my voice. They want my opinion. And my opinion comes with an attitude! One client, for example, read one of my articles in *Business Punk* and it made him laugh so hard, he knew he had to email me.

When people want to work with me, I clarify I need long deadlines because I'm traveling. I deliver on time, but I just can't do last minute requests. I refuse to work on projects that require many appointments, or even worse, back and forth emailing and too many agreements. If I have more than two appointments in a week, I get annoyed. I like writing because I can do it on my own terms, during the time of the day that suits me, not others.

Being self-employed, how do you balance your work life?

I've never traveled just for the sake of traveling. I've always worked on something. Given I work online, taking time off means I disconnect from the internet. I disconnect to reconnect, either with myself as a person or with the environment I'm in. It's become the most rewarding part of my lifestyle. Of course, it's also the most annoying part because I'm really dependent on the internet. But it's incredible to do things where you don't have access to the internet. There's a lot of time I waste just surfing the web, but the older I get, the more conscious I am of my time and how I use it. Social media is important because when you don't have office mates, you at least have people online you can talk to. But you should also draw a line to how much you make yourself available.

My goal when going freelance was not to work with assholes ever again. But if you have that attitude, you can't be an asshole to yourself. In every company, there's someone who takes care of you taking enough time off, and that's what you need to do as a freelancer. When you work late, you should start working later the next day. Treat yourself as if you're your own employee and treat others the same way. I'd never send something to my assistant at 10pm and expect to get it done by 8am the next day. If they want to work at night, that's fair, but as a principle, I wouldn't ask them to.

I always tell everyone I like to plan ahead as much as possible. I want to know the workload for each client a month or two ahead of time. Once I know that my workload for a client is four days in a month, I can plan them out as I want. If I travel, I don't plan to work. I want to take out the stress of the situation as much as possible. I also know that whenever I arrive in a new country, I need two days to adjust, so I don't plan to work on those days either. If I manage to squeeze in some work, okay, but if not, that's okay too. I want to give myself the space and time that I need to, and that's also how I set deadlines with clients, either before I fly somewhere else or at least a week after I land. I know that I don't want to work with anyone that doesn't tolerate this level of freedom.

I can work 16 hours a day if I have to, but I can also work for 30 minutes. My long-term goal is to work as little as possible. I've been looking for ways to replace myself. I've hired a virtual assistant and she takes care of a lot of things. I think about what sort of things I invest my time in because my goal is to build up as many scalable sources of income as possible.

I know it all sounds fishy because we've all heard too many times how you should start a blog to get rich, but I believe that if you learn to focus and if you think about how to invest your time in a way that benefits others the most, you'll be able to cut back on unnecessary work hours. And not just because you become much more aware of how you spend your time, but also because you'll stop spending money on things just to treat yourself. You know, those guilty pleasures that you pick up in a store after a long day at work. I just don't do that, don't even have the desire anymore!

How does it work out financially for you?
Working remotely as a freelancer does wonders for how productive you become. I get things done much faster. Thus, the presence culture where you sit at the office until late at night has never appealed to me. I really like being rewarded for what I do and not how much time I spend on doing something. I have months where I earn twice as much as I did at the office, but then I also have months where I earn half of it. Both is cool.

I need between €2,000 and €3,000 gross a month to have the lifestyle I wish to have. Mostly, I need less than that, especially when I'm not in a major European hub. While I don't spend much, I also think it's important to have a savings fund. I don't know if you've heard about the term "fuck you money," but that's pretty much my strategy. I keep money on the side so that whenever something happens, a work assignment doesn't go as planned, or when I need to leave a place earlier than I expected, I have enough on the side to do just that. I'd say having more than €10,000 is the ideal, but Tim, the friend who said I should start blogging, always says that once you have more than €2,000 in your bank account, you have nothing to complain about!

In 2016, there was a moment where my main client dropped me. It was €2,000 a month I needed to somehow replace. I was angry for a week because I knew I needed to find something else to fill the gap in my finances. I was on a cruise at that time and I spent the week staring at the ocean. There's a quote in the book *Rich Dad. Poor Dad.* that says you're rich for the time until you have to work again. I counted all the money I had left in all my bank accounts and realized I was fine. I knew that if I needed €2,000 a month, I had a few months left until I needed to look for a new client. Two weeks later, I replaced that client, but it really gave me peace of mind to know I didn't need to worry too much because of my "fuck you fund."

Being European, we're exceptionally lucky because we don't have all these student loans that hold us back. If we want to have a nomadic lifestyle, it's almost an obligation to just go for it. I don't think you'll wake up in ten years and think, "Where did that €20K go?" You'll know it went to Bali!

How do you budget for your travels?
If you calculate €50 a day and you multiply that amount by 30, you'll get to €1,500 a month. I rarely spend €50 a day because when you stay in an Airbnb in Europe, it's around €30 and then you still have €20 for food. That's actually a lot! If you're in Asia, then the money goes even further. If I stay on someone's couch, then it's as if I've saved €30. When I used to work at an office, I had moments when I'd think, "Now, I'll treat myself," and I'd go shopping. I don't have that need anymore. I don't think to myself I deserve those shoes. I'm fine with my flip flops.

If you speak German, I recommend reading Meike Winnemuth's book, *Das große Los*. It's a book she wrote after she won a million euros in a TV show and decided to explore the world. She's a journalist like me and figured out pretty quickly that she could've done it without all that extra money. There are many jobs that allow you to travel and still work and have a normal life without having to be rich.

What's something you'd recommend to others who want to travel the way you do?

Don't overthink things! And also, please stop reading all these tips on the internet! You'll never know if this lifestyle suits you unless you try it for yourself. All you really need is curiosity, a (credit) card with a nice little "fuck you" fund on it, your passport, and some extra underwear. The rest is just fear; leave it behind.

Theresa Lachner on
Web: lvstprinzip.de
Instagram: @theresa.lvstprinzip

Let's take a few moments...

· *What do you optimize your life for?*

· *Define success! What does it mean for you to be successful?*

· *Is there a way for you to measure your success?*

· *What do you need to do to reassure yourself you're successful when you're having a bad day? (Best to reply to this question when you're having an extraordinarily good day!)*

QUESTIONS

- *What's a project idea you have that you'd like to work on?*

- *Who do you need to accomplish that idea?*

- *Time to set up a project plan! I mean it!*

2

ABOUT

MINDFUL-
NESS

*I*f you've recently started your business, then working gives you pleasure. You probably don't mind sitting at your desk for 14 hours a day if there are no other responsibilities that need your attention. As a creative, it's very likely your mind never sleeps because you're constantly stimulating yourself to seek out more creative ideas. However - and this depends on what sort of person you are - there will be aspects of your business that you love and other aspects that make you feel anxious or possibly even annoyed. Once you've figured out how to make money with your beloved craft and how to run a business, you might want to start thinking about how to minimize the effort you spend on tasks you don't enjoy all that much. You might want (or even need) to figure out how to take more time off. You might want to spend time on self-development instead of on tasks that you'll essentially need to monetize. In other words, you might wish to figure out how you can make freelancing better fit your lifestyle.

When someone once asked me what I believe mindfulness was, I replied that it's the contentment with yourself and how you're spending your time in a particular moment. Or also, the recognition that things aren't going the way they should, so there's need for change that you consciously begin to implement. Mindfulness means being good to yourself and taking care of your needs. Mindfulness means living up to your personal values. However, mindfulness also means making rational decisions that are best for you and the ones around you. The biggest treat of being self-employed is that over time, you're able to choose who you want to work with. (Of course, this correlates with how well you've branded yourself for a specific industry or set of skills, and also, unfortunately, the economic situation you're in at a particular time.) Compared to working for an agency, and what has personally been a big relief is I no longer need to work with companies that contradict my personal values. I only work on projects that I believe in with people who I think are wonderful. Being at peace with the sort of work I do is what makes me satisfied with my day-to-day. At least, most of the time.

Usually, when you work on projects that you're excited about and with people you want to work with, you're more likely to deliver incredible work, and thus, word spreads. Eventually, more projects come your way, often through referrals - in the most ideal cases, anyway. In a less ideal one, there will be long stretches of time without much work to keep you busy, and your bank account might not be in a state that allows for a good night's sleep.

Given that as a freelancer, you're mostly dependent on being hired externally, so there are times where you'll have more work than you can potentially handle and other times where there won't be much to do. This is one of the reasons why I stressed the idea of initiating your own projects and then finding ways to monetize them when writing *My Creative (Side) Business*. What I'd like to mention at this stage (and before I forget) is that each industry has its busy and more relaxed seasons. Once you've worked as a freelancer for several years, you should be able to recognize when there won't be any work coming your way, so make the most of the free time! Michèle talks more about this sort of time management in her interview.

In the following chapter and on the following pages, I'll describe different aspects of being mindful regarding your career. As a freelancer, you're likely to be by yourself a lot, and also in your own head, so I'll try to address different aspects of mindfulness that many of the ladies mentioned during our conversations.

Now, are you sitting comfortably? Gosh, I'd love to see where you're sitting right now. It's such a joy knowing that someone, you, is sitting somewhere in the world reading these pages!

1 KNOW YOURSELF, TRUST YOURSELF

When you first decided to jump into freelancing, you probably knew it wouldn't be easy, but you had the confidence in yourself that you'd eventually make it. You were willing to give up the assurance of a regular paycheck. You knew you wouldn't be fully independent from day one, but you were sure you'd get there!

You should definitely give yourself a high-five for having that sort of confidence in your ability! It takes a lot of courage to acknowledge and respect your skills and capabilities. Especially because many people will tell you all sorts of things to question or doubt yourself. However – and you should always remember this, even if you've heard this a million times already – these people are showing you their limitations, not yours. Because, quite frankly, if you're willing to put in the effort and are willing to work on your skills with determination, then you can solve whatever challenges you've set out for yourself.

It takes a lot of imagination to make self-employment work, especially now with the internet where things are changing almost every day. What might've worked yesterday might not work tomorrow, so you need to make an extra effort to stay on top of current trends and changes in your industry, while also keeping up appearances to get hired for your unique style. Additionally, it's not easy dreaming up where the journey should go. Discovering a project you could self-initiate to meet your ambition can be challenging, in addition to managing the usual life stuff that comes your way to distract you from what you'd like to be working on. (Sometimes.) To me, freelancing often feels like a crazy rush; a high, like I imagine drugs to be. When things are going well, there's this almost ecstatic excitement, but simulta-neously, I feel like I'm in a car that's going too fast and I'm horrified to lose control of it. In other words, it's the fear that a project might fall through, or a client I wanted to work with rejects my efforts for some reason I might not understand in that moment.

I've learned to gain control and became more easy-going about my fears, compared to when I was working for a startup a couple of years ago. There, I was never truly sure if the company would still exist the next month, so I needed to take time to reflect on what exactly it was that caused my anxiety. Even though I still sometimes hear the linger-ing voice in the back of my head saying, "What if things don't work out?", I've learned how to deal with it over time.

What helped was asking myself how I'd feel if this project wasn't there anymore; if someone took away a certain chance. I realized how much of my identity depends on working for a particular company or client. I can only keep up my self-confidence if I'm in control of what my identity relates to. Now, I try to find a way to replace the feeling, the identity boost, that a project I'm not in control of could give me. Often, I want to see projects work out because it's projects I identify with, I'd love to work on, and it's something I'd like to tell others I've contributed to. However, I also know that sometimes it's better to take matters in my own hands and focus my energy on projects I have full control of.

Turning down a client is naturally easier when you have enough money in your bank account. However, it does pay off to risk it, turn down projects you wouldn't be fully invested in, and work on some-thing that gives you not just a great reference, but also something to talk about with pride and excitement. Down the road, it's much better to have a portfolio filled with projects you think are wonderful than to gather references that might've paid the bills, but you were indifferent about.

Of course, it's also never too late to switch gears and start building a portfolio in the direction you wish if what you've done up until now doesn't quite suit where you see yourself in the future. At the end of the day, your website is nothing more than a wishlist of what you want to work on in the future, supported with relatable references from the past.

When you think about yourself as a freelancer, you should also think about what sort of clients and projects you want to be associated with. On one hand, it'll make it easier to say "no" and prioritize client requests, should you get too many. On the other hand, it'll be easier to create your own projects to build a portfolio you're excited about. If you're someone who gets excited like a puppy because you can fall in love with the potential for any sort of project, you'll need to learn to become pragmatic and accept that your day only has 24 hours. If you run into working overtime a lot and you burn yourself out because you're in high demand and no longer have time for things you'd like to be doing, you'll have to be stricter with yourself and be really conscious of your values. At the end of the day, you're just a human being and simply can't do it all. It also goes without saying: you need to plan leisure time, even if you're trying to overcome personal troubles and use your work as a distraction. It's something I'm guilty of myself as I often tempt to use work as a way to escape the troubles of my personal life and lose myself in projects.

If, of course, you don't have this problem and consider me a lunatic while reading these pages, that's okay! But if you find yourself relating to this struggle, it might be worthwhile to schedule regular times to work on your business, think about your business model, and how you can build additional sources of income.

From my personal experience, and what I've heard from others when interviewing them, learning to say "no" is a big step for every freelancer. If you've been building your portfolio of references strategically, sooner or later, there will be a point when you'll have to learn to turn down requests. At best, when you feel like something isn't a project for you, you should turn it down immediately, especially if a project came through a referral because it sheds a bad light on them if they recommend someone who's not reliable.

When talking to Liz, she expressed that in order for her to accept work, it has to tick at least two out of three boxes; those boxes being easy, interesting, and/or well-paid. I'd add that you should only accept work you trust will enhance your portfolio. If you don't feel it would, let it go. If you want it or not, it's always your choice what projects and activities you'll fill your time with! Make them matter!

2 EMBRACE THE CHOICES YOU HAVE

The moment you decided to go freelance, you decided to create an everyday that's full of choices. The choice of when you'll get up. The choice of where you'll work from. The choice of who you'll work with. The choice of when and for how long you'll go on vacation. Most importantly, the choice of how much you'll ask in return for your time, services, and products you create to enable you to live the life you want. There's probably a million more choices for you to consider, so when you compare it to full-time employment where someone gives you a workspace, a timesheet, a list of tasks, and an idea of how and when you should accomplish those tasks, it's quite the difference!

Having all these choices might feel overwhelming at times. Feeling obligated to favor some choices over others might feel daunting and allowing yourself to claim the choices you feel are worth pursuing requires courage. However, once you've recognized that having the freedom of choice is the ultimate benefit of the security you've given up, you'll eventually feel much more content about your situation, even in times when the roller coaster rolls downhill. As long as you believe in yourself or have the confidence to ask someone for help, you'll be fine!

The point is, you have the choice at all times and it's your responsibility, given you're your own boss, to make the necessary decisions. It's much easier to feel content if you feel like you're on top of your business; if you feel like you're the one in charge. But, for you to feel like you're just that, you need to make conscious decisions about your business that essentially fit your personality and chosen lifestyle.

Some of the decisions you'll have to make won't be the most ideal or the sort of "dream" choices, but rather necessary evils. It's part of life. Some decisions will be easy to justify and easy to make. For some decisions, you may receive questioning looks. Other decisions might be really hard. It's important for you to take enough time to think and decide, whatever the result may be. Consider the act of making decisions an important part of your job, a part of being a freelancer. Also, remember that with decisions, you'll learn. Some mistakes will be expensive, but it's as if you're paying into your school of life fund. It's all okay.

When conducting interviews for *This Year Will Be Different*, Oren Lasry mentioned that you must not just work "in" your business, but also "on" your business. Working "on" your business should make up about 50% of your time commitment. That sort of thinking led me to focus on building scalable income streams when researching for *My Creative (Side) Business*. What I believe is an important part of *Work Trips and Road Trips*, and what I hope you'll take away from reading these pages, is that you'll make time to think about the sort of decisions you need to make. Not just the day-to-day decisions, but also the hard ones that will make you feel like the captain of your ship.

Many freelancers often wonder if they should get another job when things become challenging. It feels like the easy way out. It's safe when you have someone else telling you what to do. Those opportunities feel really exciting before you realize that with every job, you won't just get the great parts: a paycheck and a regular vacation. You'll also have to deal with the downsides, which, funnily enough, are similar to the upsides: a paycheck and a regular vacation. (We'll get to that in more detail later.) Plus, you'll also have a daily commute, most likely during rush hour. You'll only have time for quick lunches, and there won't be spontaneous coffee breaks with friends in the middle of the day on a random Thursday.

I remember this one moment where I decided to give up one of my clients, which at that time was my main source of income. I mostly did it with the goal to make space for new opportunities and because my work became very repetitive and tiring. Around the same time, a big tech company started advertising in my Facebook feed that they were hiring. I clicked on the ad and found myself sucked into the career page where I found a really interesting position based out of London. Being the excited puppy I am and seeing all the possibilities, I immediately started crafting an application letter. The next day, I needed to take the subway during rush hour, so it was then that I realized if I got the job, that would pretty much be my everyday life. I suddenly knew that I didn't need to look for a job. I needed to do some soul-searching and think about what I actually wanted out of my life; what I wanted to achieve. I had to discover how I wanted to contribute and most importantly, how I wanted my day-to-day to be like. Also, I needed to understand what steps I needed to take to feel a sense of direction again, the sort of direction that seemed to have gone missing. At least, temporarily.

There aren't that many jobs where you can do whatever comes to your mind. Being a freelancer, however, is one of the jobs that actually allows you to do just about anything that fits your skills and measures up to your ambitions. Deciding to become a freelancer, you've built the engine to take you wherever you want to go. The really hard decision is, where is that?

When I registered my company in 2014, I remember a good friend told me, "Welcome to the game!" Now, three years later, I actually understand what he meant. I'm the person who decides what it means to win and what it means to lose. I'm the person that makes the rules to work, play, and live by. There will always be obstacles, as there are in every game you play, but it's the feeling you get from conquering those that make you go higher and feel the rush, the excitement and the awe of what you've accomplished! (Which is also why you should celebrate and why you should celebrate often!)

If you don't set the rules and if you don't make up a framework, it will be much harder in the long-term to enjoy yourself. It will be much harder to pick yourself up when you've lost a sense of direction. Each game has its rules, and the most exciting games even have levels that push you to rise up and above. What you need to do is decide what those rules are. You need to define your levels and generally make a game plan. This isn't about deciding where you'll be in a week, a month, or a year. Physically, anyway. This is far more about consciously paying attention to your definition of success. It's thinking about how you'll promote yourself. And it's also about defining what sort of skills you want to learn and how you'll measure your progress!

3 DARE TO BE INDEPENDENT

In *My Creative (Side) Business*, I touched on the difference between building a creative business and being a freelancer. As a creative entrepreneur, you build a company with multiple income streams. You build a business that's bigger than you, which, in my definition, doesn't mean that you necessarily need to hire people. As a freelancer, you work towards a client's goal. You're a service provider and once your services are no longer needed, you move on to another client.

In my theory, part of being a creative entrepreneur means thinking about how to replace yourself so that earning money – and your earning potential in general – isn't directly correlated with the time you spend actively working on a task. Some people build a business by hiring people. Then, they spend most of their time working "on" their business as they have people who work "in" their business. However, employing people means carrying full responsibility for others. The success of the company depends on your ability to find paying customers so you can then pay your team. Do you really want that sort of obligation? If the answer is "yes," then that's great! If, however, the answer is "no" but you just don't know how else to deal with the growing demand for your services, hiring still might not be the right answer for you.

Different people I talked to had different approaches. Laura, for example, whose story you'll read in the section about money, founded a collective; a group of solopreneurs that all source for assignments and collaborate whenever they need help. Because Laura has established her own signature style, many people who come to her are happy to wait to have her create the look and feel of their companies. She tempts to work with the people within her collective and she enjoys teamwork, so being part of a collective is highly beneficial. Simultaneously, she doesn't want or need to commit to taking care of employees, looking for projects she might not be passionate about just to pay everyone. She only works with fellow freelancers and thus, everyone keeps their personal freedom. She also has people she can recommend whenever she doesn't want to or can't take on a project. Liz, whose story you'll dive into in the travel section, has increased her rates. She either takes on higher-paying clients, or clients with a smaller budget because it's fun, easy, and fast to do. Theresa is also a great example. You've read her story while reading about success. She hired a virtual assistant, a fellow freelancer, that takes care of all sorts of tasks for her, from booking flights to responding to emails. That gives Theresa more time to focus on what she wants to spend her time on: writing. If you remember the stories from *My Creative (Side) Business*, many of the women I interviewed focused on producing content that they then sold through companies and lived off of royalties. There's no right or wrong way to run a business. There are different attitudes to building a business while remaining independent. What's important is to build a business that suits your needs and serves your lifestyle.

Finding purpose, on the other hand, is mostly about defining who you want to serve. It's not as much about what you want to do with your time, but much more about how you want to contribute to your community. It's about asking yourself who the people are you want to serve with your products and services? What problems are you solving and why? Knowing or having the conscious awareness of how you want to be spending your days will give you the confidence to know what sort of projects are right or wrong for you, despite your current workload.

Being independent gives you the possibility to be agile. It's easier to say "no" to projects that don't fit who you are if you're the only person dependent on your income. It's easier to live up to your morals and pursue projects you really want to work on if you don't have to make sure your employees get paid on time. Nevertheless, it's easier to feel a sense of purpose if you're taking care of other people instead of searching for what fills your own soul with purpose and a sense of direction, which is why the state of, "Should I look for another job?" might come up from time to time.

Asking yourself all sorts of questions is important. It's also important that you review whether working as you do in a given moment is the right form for you to work. I'd call this everyday soul-searching; I really believe that while you should set higher goals and be aware of why you're doing what you're doing, you should also pay attention to how you want to be spending your days. Because, I'll say it again, you're the one who must define that! You should feel accomplished because you're good to yourself, and you take the time to live a life that allows you to be present and savor the moments as they are.

What I like about freelancing is that it gives you the necessary space to define and redefine yourself day after day. It's the perfect framework to do whatever you want to be doing and how you want to be doing it. Then again, you should know that it's also possible to change that. You don't always have to go straight ahead; you can also go sideways.

If you no longer want to do what you're doing, you might want to gather all your courage and end the relationship with your best-paying client. You might want to rebrand your business. You might feel like moving to a different location or going nomadic for a while. It's in your own hands and you should take the time to reflect on what suits you. Then, make changes when something doesn't suit you anymore. Gather your courage to break out of your routine from time to time, and make space to do something that will challenge you or will make you feel promoted, despite what others say, even if they tell you you're crazy.

Trust me, you got this!

4 ENHANCE RUNNING A SOLOPRENEUR BUSINESS

———

Generally speaking, the bigger the problem you're trying to solve or the longer a project takes, the longer it will take for you to accomplish a task. Not to mention, the longer it will take for you to feel like you've accomplished something, like you're moving forward.

It's necessary you determine what it takes to reassure yourself you're on the right track to feel adept. If the stretches between taking on a project and having the feeling of accomplishment are longer than what you can naturally tolerate to feel at ease, you might have to find ways to create such feedback loops.

With business models that are spun around working only on other people's projects, it's harder to ensure you'll get feedback the way you need to feel like your work matters. Being a service provider, the acknowledgment for your work doesn't always come in ways you need to receive it, so you might get temporarily, and maybe even increasingly, dissatisfied. Should you notice that creeping feeling in the back of your head, think about what would give you the coveted self-esteem boost and pursue that too. I'm saying "too" because you might need to take on certain projects to pay your bills, however, you might also have to regularly help your portfolio of work evolve in the direction you want it to. If you offer your services to a company as a freelancer, then there's no HR department and no manager to think about the development of your career. A company that hired you as a freelancer hired you so you could get a job done for them. They didn't hire you to offer a stepping stone. They can be a stepping stone, but you must be the one to think about how to make your freelancing experience with them be one. How you can make yourself grow and what you want to achieve next! If you freelance for a company, they still don't look out for your personal development. They look at their checks and balances. If you do your job well, they won't risk promoting you because they'd have to find someone to replace you. And if you do your job well but need a new challenge, it won't be your client helping you make those moves. You'll have to figure out what you need to do to promote yourself in order to grow.

Usually as a freelancer, you get hired for tasks because someone has seen your work for another client or your credentials, and they want you to – more or less – replicate that success. While it's great when referrals land in your lap, it's important to think about your personal development and, from time to time, make space in your busy schedule to sit down and reflect about what you need to do that would let you recognize you've promoted yourself. Looking to the future and thinking about what you're building and why you're doing what you're doing is a big part of running a company. It's the power and the curse of being a solopreneur because there's simply no one else to deal with these questions. It's been discussed many times that not everyone has a higher goal or knows what sort of company they want to build. But even if you're a freelancer, a service provider, you still run a company, one way or another. It's perfectly fine to work towards the success of others, but you should also define smaller projects that make your company a company. In order to grow and enhance your business, you should make up projects that enable you to learn and grow in a more self-directed way. It could be projects that you might eventually be able to monetize. (I've talked enough about this in *My Creative (Side) Business* already.) However, and to get things straight, when I talk about self-initiated projects, I don't mean you need to publish a best seller tomorrow or have your paintings hang at the MoMa next week. It's enough to create a series of illustrations and sell them at a local market if it's something you haven't done yet. Think of a first step. Think of something that might take a couple of weeks to set up. Then, eventually, you might have a fixed shelf space at a local store. Something that might take a few months to figure out how to do. And one day, if you remain focused, you'll hopefully feel confident enough to submit your illustrations to a major publisher to go along with the words of your favorite writer. Something that might have felt out of reach when you first sat behind a stand at the neighborhood crafts market. This, of course, might take a couple of years, maybe decades to set up, but it's the sort of progress that will allow you to feel accomplished, even in times when clients don't come running through the door. Through self-initiated projects, you'll be kept on your toes, have something to attach your identity to, and you'll learn new ways to build a sustainable business. Generally speaking, you need to think and make plans for how you'll grow as a professional in the long run. It's just like when you have a job and grow bored with it, you'd start looking for a new one to seek out new challenges. Being a freelancer, you shouldn't look for a new job unless you really want one, or a job that you're crazy about falls into your lap. If you feel the crippling feeling and the need to do something new, reassess the projects you're working on first. If a project no longer suits your personality, you might want to look for new projects as if you'd be looking for a new position with a different company.

Saying goodbye to Kickstarter as a client after two years was an incredibly hard decision for me to make. Nevertheless, I didn't doubt for just a second it was a decision necessary for me to make. I simply wanted and needed to make space for new challenges and experiences. And I wanted to have more time for my personal projects. Self-initiated projects make the difference between being a freelancer and being a creative entrepreneur. It's the difference between working towards the success of other people compared to working on something that's bigger than yourself. As a freelancer, you can define your progress by working with clients that are more interesting to you or that pay better, but you're still working towards something where you'll never be able to take full ownership. It's having full ownership that usually leads to feeling more content and satisfied.

5 RECHARGE YOUR BATTERIES

———

Are you exhausted from everything I've mentioned to think about and consider in your day-to-day? All of the decisions you'll have to make? I bet! As motivated as I feel every time I reread my words, I also feel as though everything I've written can make one slightly tired. The good (and the bad) news is that there's one other responsibility I haven't mentioned yet, but probably made you curious when you picked up this book: the responsibility to take enough breaks!

Given you're an entrepreneur, there's understandably always something for you to do. If you don't determine how much work is enough work and how much money is enough money, you could most certainly work day and night. While many people decide to freelance so they can free themselves from the defined structure of a 9-to-5 job, sooner or later, many realize that building a business might keep them busier behind their desk for much longer than a regular job.

It helps to have thought about your values and having made a game plan to follow whenever you're faced with hard decisions. The more specific you are about what you want your solopreneur life to be, how you want to live and work, the easier it will be to look for pragmatic solutions to fit that framework. When you define how much you want to work and how much you want to earn, you'll be able to understand how to best build a framework to live up to your ideal freelancer being.

Being mindful in the context of freelancing, to come back to the overall theme of this chapter, means several things: it's about accepting the client work you believe in. It's about self-initiating the projects you'd like to be known for. It's about knowing when to say "no." It's

about acknowledging that you're a human being who seeks confir-
mation, and looking for ways to receive that sort of affirmation in a
form that makes you feel like your work matters. However, it's also
about making sure you give yourself enough time and space away
from working to keep whatever you produce fresh and exciting. Being
mindful is about figuring out what you want to learn and making sure
you make space for just that. It's living up to your values and giving
yourself the space and the freedom to shift priorities if necessary.

Now, while I've spent this chapter talking a lot about managing your
business thoughtfully, I haven't made much space to talk about how
to take breaks. I mostly rely on the interviews to give you inspiration
for how to manage your resources: time, energy, and finances.

But let me just say this: it's understandable that freelancing is something most jump into with enthusiasm, and that's why planning for
breaks often gets overlooked. Once you get used to a fast-paced life
filled with work, it's hard to tap on the brakes to make yourself slow
down, unless something is groundbreaking and forces you to do so.

It's especially difficult to draw a line when you have the internet at
your fingertips. At least part of your work is likely to be in the cloud and
available from anywhere, even on your smartphone. Many people I've
talked to embrace not having structure when they first started out as
freelancers, but sooner or later realized they needed to make up some
rules to make time for free time. Some, such as Vicky, whose story you
might've read in *This Year Will Be Different*, rented an office space to
draw a geographic line between work and play. Laura, whose story
you'll read in the section about money, bought herself a second laptop without installing any design software to make sure she doesn't
get lured into work after her working hours are over. I no longer access
emails on my phone. At first, I switched off notifications on my phone
and no longer let emails trickle in throughout the day. Instead, I had
to open the app and request them, but now, I only read emails on
my laptop. It's a small thing, but it really changed how I make myself
available to outside impulses.

The main point of this part of the book has been to inspire you to think about the hard questions. (You'll find some at the end of this chapter.) Before you turn the page, please remember that whatever you think is the right way now, might not be the right way tomorrow. As you'll read in Becky's interview, it's perfectly fine to shift your priorities at any time.

*T*he emphasis on the preciousness of each and every moment is what I looked for when choosing the three interviews to accompany this part of the book about mindfulness.

When I spoke to Lauren Hom, a letterer and illustrator, I especially cherished her story about how she parted from all her possessions. She recognized that stuff was no longer what mattered to her. She wanted to know how people in other places lived their lives and what made them happy. She felt like the time was now to leave her safe space and make the world her teacher. Lauren has my deepest respect for following her heart and making each and every day a memorable one.

The consciousness of the presence and the ability to resist everyday distractions to savor moments as they come is what touched me when talking to Michèle Pauty, a photographer and wonderfully artistic friend of mine. Maybe some years ago, this wouldn't be as significant as it is now, but in today's world, navigating around technology and cherishing life as it unfolds in front of us is what made me introduce Michèle's story to you here.

The ability to distinguish between what matters the most in a moment and the willingness to shift priorities, regardless of what's supposedly the right thing to do, was what made Becky Burton's story so notable to me. Becky is a consultant and a writer, which might also be why her final edits of our conversation touched me to tears. Her mindfulness of what's important and prioritizing her personal values is what I find so incredibly admirable about her.

If you wake up tomorrow feeling like you can do anything and you recognize that it's in your hands to navigate through life fearlessly, then I know I made the right selection to accompany this part of the book. Savor the moments of getting to know Lauren, Michèle, and Becky.

LAUREN HOM

MAKE IT A GREAT DAY.
THE CHOICE IS YOURS,

What's been your educational and professional path?

I studied Visual Arts in New York. I always wanted to become an artist, and even though my parents were very supportive, they told me (by a standard narrative) that as an artist, I'd be very poor. I then majored in Advertising because it seemed like the intersection between practicality and creativity.

For about nine months after graduation, I worked for an advertising agency, and on the side, I was freelancing for some smaller assignments and illustrating for fun. I always shared my work online, which turned out to be crucial. I started a blog called *The Daily Dishonesty* that became very popular and gave me a lot of followers.

As an entry-level art director, it usually takes a few years to work yourself up. You don't start with the most exciting projects, so I would come home and often feel exhausted. I thought to myself, "I'm 23 and I'm tired. I'm not supposed to be tired. I'm supposed to be full of life! How on earth are you supposed to work in a job for forty years if you feel like this after just about six months?!"

Luckily, from having all these work references online, a lot of people wanted to work with me. I left my full-time job because I knew I could fill my time, and if I worked hard and dedicated all my energy to making it work as a freelance illustrator, I could eventually make a living from it. Once you dare to make such a leap and leave your safety net behind, it really puts you into survivor mode. Right before I left my full-time job, I contacted several illustration representatives. At that time, I was 23 and honestly had no idea what I was doing. I just thought that having an agent would make me look more credible, and retrospectively, it really did.

Finding an agent didn't take too long. I looked at the websites of the illustrators I admire, checked out their contact pages, and approached their agents. I sent my portfolio to about twenty agencies, then I heard back from five or six. Sometimes, an agent won't take you if your work is too familiar to that of someone else they represent, or if they simply think they can't help you find good clients. Then, you just need to keep trying! One agent, one of my favorites actually, decided to take a chance on me and signed me up, even though I didn't have too many references at that time. My biggest project I had done to date was some signage for the Dallas Fort Worth airport. Now I work with clients like Starbucks, AT&T, and Google.

How is your business set up?
I've been freelancing since 2013. At the beginning, a lot of the assignments came through my blog and social media. My work was just very visible on the internet. Now, about 90% of my income is from contract illustration work. I work on a per project basis with clients. I illustrate advertising campaigns, greeting cards ... anything that needs lettering really. You might not realize how many things need lettering, but it goes from beauty products, to T-shirts; anything you see that has letters on it has been designed by someone!

I still remember how I got my first job. It was a spread for a magazine and what I didn't know at that time was all the magazine art directors keep an eye on what other magazines are up to. Once that tiny publication hit the stands, I quickly got requests from five or six other magazines to do illustration work for them. It went from there.

I also teach online courses, which gives me some extra income each month. And when I go to new places, I might teach a workshop there, which I announce on social media. How much I work often depends on the project I'm working on. Sometimes, I have regular, 40-hour weeks, and other weeks, I don't work at all. When push comes to shove, I don't have a hard time buckling down and getting things done. But client work can be quite sporadic, so I have a lot of personal projects. If I don't work, then I get really antsy after about three weeks. I need to do something productive at least once a day to feel content. I draw in my sketchbook or look for other ways to be creative. Even if I'm not working, I'm actually still working.

Having an agent means I don't have to do any of the negotiations or administrative work. I don't have to deal with contracts! I can fully focus on being creative, and that's worth the fee they're getting. I'm a big fan of outsourcing the work you're not the best at. I'm not great at paperwork, so I'd rather pay someone to do it for me. Working the way I do, I don't have to worry about picking up the phone. I can just immerse myself in new places, at least as long as I find joy in doing it and deliver my work on time.

How would you describe your attitude towards travel?
I hit the road in January 2016. After living in New York for seven years, I had pretty much everything at my disposal. You can press some buttons on your phone and order anything from pizza to ice cream. You become quite spoiled. I didn't want to have that sort of lifestyle anymore, so I decided to sell everything and travel the world with no more than a backpack.

It was more or less the same decision process as with quitting my job. One morning, I woke up and I thought to myself, I could be anywhere in the world, why am I in New York? At the age of 25, I thought this was the time to try new things. I figured, when will I ever have the possibility to travel so freely ever again? I knew that living with less would also give me a greater appreciation for when I decide to nest up again.

I realized it would take forever to sell everything I owned one by one. Already putting a price tag on everything you own takes forever, and probably makes you cogitate about all your things and your emotional connection to them too! Instead, I decided to make something that can be best described as an "All-You-Can-Eat-Buffet-Style-Yard-Sale." I put all my clothes and my art supplies out and opened my doors from 9am until 8pm on a Sunday. It was "all you can take for $30." I think I made something like $1,000. It was fun to watch things go, but there were definitely some items where I struggled. I also had something like 40 pairs of shoes, and let's be honest, no one needs 40 pairs of shoes. It was a good exercise.

I never considered myself a very materialistic person, and I thought that there probably won't be too many moments in my life where I'll be able to get rid of all my stuff. One of the reasons I'm traveling is because it makes me constantly redefine what it means to be happy and what it means to be successful. After seven years of living in a big city, such as New York or LA, any city that's business-minded really, you get a pretty good sense of what it means to be happy and successful. I needed to challenge that.

Working 70 hours, which to many seems normal, and hustling really hard to be able to go out, buy expensive meals, and pay $2,000 for rent seemed so normal there. I just wanted to pop that bubble. I wanted to see how people in places, such as Copenhagen or Budapest, felt about success. What being happy meant to them.

Being a designer, I do miss curating my own little space, and living with six dresses, two tops, two skirts, and two pairs of shoes is a radical opposite to how my life used to be, but it's been really great! I must admit, I've been able to pack so lightly because on my travels, I chase good weather around the globe. One day when I'm older, I'll have more responsibilities and I'm sure I'll be tied down to a place, but where my life is at now, I feel like it's time to experiment with different lifestyles.

How did you start implementing travel into your work life after you went freelance?

As a freelance illustrator, I've always worked from home, so it's not as if anything besides the time zones changed how I work. Sometimes, I end up working with a client during their hours, which might be in the middle of the night for me. But other times, it's fairly flexible and I can just work regular hours. That's the advantage of project-based work.

I must admit, I had a hard time focusing when I first began freelancing, simply because you can sleep until whenever you want. You can do whatever you want. It's such a paradox because so many seem to chase the idea of freelancing and having complete freedom, but once you have that sort of freedom, you crave structure.

After some time freelancing out of my bedroom in New York, I was planning to travel with one of my best friends, but a couple of months before our planned departure, she got her dream job and decided not to join me. It was a bummer! There I was with my big plans, all by myself! I then found out about the Remote Year, a program where you travel around the world with a group of like-minded people. The organization takes care of all the logistics, such as booking flights or accommodations, and you're surrounded by a community. It seemed perfect because while I wanted to travel, I didn't want to travel by myself. I hadn't done any solo traveling before and I didn't feel comfortable hitting the road for so long on my own. I, too, had my preconceptions about traveling around the world solo as a female, so joining Remote Year felt like a good way to get travel sea legs before I'd have the courage to travel alone. I dropped out after a couple of months because I felt ready to travel by myself much earlier than expected. After five months, I gave the team at the Remote Year program a two-month notice I was leaving so there wouldn't be any bad blood. While it was nice to have someone else do all the planning, it's also nice to do it myself for a change.

How do you tell your clients you're working on the road?
When I talk to my clients, I only talk with them about the creative

work and how to best implement their feedback. Everything else, all of the contracts and negotiations, are done by my agent. Once a contract is signed, my agent puts me in touch with the client. Before I had my agent, I found myself managing the kind of relationship where you're working with somebody and you have a good creative flow, you're great with all the creative things, and then all of a sudden, you must talk money. I struggled with the duality of those two things. I prefer to just talk creative to the people I work with.

My clients know I'm on the road. When I work on a 48-hour deadline, I tell them where I am and make sure I deliver on time.

One of the reasons I decided to leave New York was because most of my clients didn't care where I was. It's not like an illustrator gets paid more just because they live in NYC. It really is your work that matters.

Being self-employed, how do you balance your work life?
My work schedule is variable. Sometimes, I don't take full days off. I take segments of hours off. If I work on a big project, I might work a lot. Then, work might get sporadic and I don't work for weeks. Earlier in 2016, I had a month where I didn't get a single paying client. I started to get concerned and nervous, but then work came in again. Because work gets sporadic at times, I tend to say "yes" to a lot of things.

Sometimes, I might not have any assignments, but then I still draw in my sketchbook, do my side projects, and share a lot of what I create online. My parents raised me to be very practical with money, so before I left for the round trip, I had quite a bit of savings. I know that even if something catastrophic would happen, I'd still be okay.

A lot of people assume that if you live a nomadic lifestyle, you're on an infinite vacation. That's definitely not true! It's one of the challenges to find a balance between enjoying a new city and getting enough work done. Sometimes, you have to stay in and work all day, even though there's sun outside and you'd much rather explore, but then you can work around the sunny hours and buckle down at night instead of the afternoon.

It's a different experience to travel like a digital nomad because you have to accept that you won't see all the different tourist attractions. It's still a normal work day. I often get in my head and think about what I'm *supposedly* supposed to be doing. However, you must also realize, you need to do whatever you need to do at that time and focus on that. It's okay! The grass will always be greener on the other side and social media multiplies that feeling. Sometimes, you need to remind yourself you're not on vacation and that while you need to keep your head down and work today, it's okay because of the long-term benefit of traveling and working the way you chose to.

How does it work out financially for you?
My projects range anywhere from $500 to $25,000, so I need to get a couple of the $25,000 assignments once in awhile. When I was traveling with the Remote Year, I had to pay them $2,000 a month for accommodation, a work space, and the plane ticket between countries. My budget's less now because I stay in an Airbnb or at friends' places.

I've always been very thrifty and I'm really good at saving money. It's interesting because my parents taught us to save, but I then had to learn how to allow myself to spend the money I've been earning. I have a tendency to hoard for rainy days, but really, what's the point of not going out for that meal because you could, quite frankly, also die tomorrow? What's the point of working if you can't enjoy the benefits? I think I definitely have about a year-worth of earnings set aside. Just in case something went terribly wrong, I know I'd be okay, but I also have to remind myself to spend the money because it's what I've earned.

A big advantage of being a digital nomad and earning in USD or Euro is that you can make your money work for you more if you live in a city where the currency isn't as strong. You might be making

$50K, which in New York, doesn't get you far, but in Prague or Budapest, your spending power is suddenly much higher!

Even though I'm spending less than I used to in New York, the quality of my life has increased significantly. It sounds so cliché to say that, but if you want to travel with fewer things, you'll end up with more. I'm definitely saving so much because I spend so much less and on top of everything, I'm just as happy, if not more, than when I was living in New York.

I try to save about 40% of what I make. I live super frugally. I wouldn't consider myself a budget traveler, but I just don't buy a lot of stuff and now that I live out of a backpack, I spend even less. It's something that I find so incredibly fascinating about the lifestyle of a digital nomad. Even if you're not doing something creative for a living, you'll train yourself to be more creative and think outside the box. There's something that forces you to think alternatively.

Over the past couple of years, I've been trying to become more financially savvy. Besides having a business bank account, a regular savings account, a retirement account, and some small investments, I haven't yet figured out how to "grow" money. If you just keep money in your savings account, it depreciates in value over time because of inflation, which is like the digital equivalent of keeping money under your mattress. When I started traveling, I went through a mindset shift, thinking more about long-term goals instead of short-term pleasures. I'm still figuring out how I'll invest money in the future.

How do you budget for your trips?
I don't budget. I just don't spend a lot and I make good money. My biggest expenses right now are flights and food. I cook a lot, so that's one thing where I save compared to others. I'm a vegetarian, so I make a lot of my own meals, a lot of salads, mostly because I like to know what I put into my body. I also pack a lot of snacks and I don't spend much money throughout the day on food. Once in awhile, I'll go out for a nice meal, but most days I cook.

I've always loved cooking, and having control of what goes into my food has been one of my favorite things. I go to farmers markets and buy fresh foods and vegetables for smoothies and salads. It's like my happy place. That's also why I stay in Airbnbs; you always have a kitchen! However, I've learned that you can also get creative and make salads in a hotel room. If you have a small refrigerator and a couple of utensils, you can tear up some veggies, put them in a tupperware, and make some really good food. I don't get emotional about these utensils either. Because I don't have space in my backpack, I've often left these new things that I bought behind for the people who come after me or that I was staying with, and then I buy new bowls and tupperware upon arrival in a new town.

Another way I save is that I pretty much exclusively shop at thrift stores. When I was 16, I used to go to charity stores and I'd buy dresses, fix them up on my mother's sewing machine, and then sell them on our front lawn. I would make about $500 or $600 each month doing that; a lot of money for a 16 year old! And I saved it! Not much has changed about my attitude. I buy secondhand. Plus, it's not like I can buy much these days. My backpack is smashed to the brim. There's only space for the bare essentials, so if I want to buy something, I need to let go of something. I can't even buy something and then ship it to my storage because I have no storage. Slowing down the buying process has felt extraordinarily healthy. Now, I really think about what's an asset in my life. I can recommend the book *The Life Changing Magic of Tidying Up* by Marie Kondo to anyone who wants to give this a go. It teaches you to get rid of everything that doesn't bring you joy.

What's something you'd recommend to others who want to travel the way you do?
You'll probably prioritize different things at different moments in your life. Changing your priorities as they change for you is perfectly fine. Nothing is black and white. It's okay to go this way and then another.

With joining the Remote Year, one thing was very interesting. I really enjoyed seeing how different people packed. Some brought four suitcases, other people brought empty suitcases because they knew they wanted to shop as they traveled the world, and others, such as myself, came just with a small backpack. Everyone's got different preferences and there's no right or wrong way. The one thing we ended up thinking, and what helped me a lot, is that at the end of the day, things are just things and whether you have too much or not enough, you can always leave stuff behind. You can give things away or you can buy more of what you need. And like I said, what you need actually isn't that much. If you're thinking about selling everything you own, do it! It's a good thing.

Lauren Hom on
Web: homsweethom.com
Instagram: @homsweethom

MICHÈLE PAUTY

TURN OFF YOUR PHONE,
YOU'RE NOT MISSING

ANYTHING

What's been your educational and professional path?

It took a while for me to find out what I wanted to study. At first, I took classes in German and Japanese Studies, and on the side I worked in a theatre. While I found my studies interesting, I also realized they weren't creative enough. But I didn't know what else to do! I just knew that I wanted to do something creative.

I participated in several entrance examinations just to see how I liked the various assignments. Then, with photography, the exam felt very different from all the other ones because for the first time, I was voluntarily investing more time. I went way beyond what was expected. Completely drawn to photography, I realized that was what I was meant to be doing!

To this day, my profession has been a real calling. There's no separation between work and life. It really is just me doing what I love. There are a lot of preconceptions of photographers being starving artists. I felt certain reservations myself at first. It was hard for me to imagine I'd one day be able to make a living like this.

After I graduated, I found a way to step into the industry by working as a staff photographer at a local newspaper before taking the plunge and going freelance! What really came in handy at my job was that I met a lot of people. Many of them liked the photographs I took of them and asked for a private studio appointment. Press photography as such has never been a long-term goal for me. In the end, I was much more intrigued by the chance of shooting portraits. Getting close to people.

I like to take time for the person I photograph in order to capture their real nature. Time isn't necessarily something you have when you constantly think of a deadline of the editorial closing. After about three years, I cut down to only work four days a week. I wanted to dedicate at least one day a week to my side projects and work with my own clients. At first, it was just for fun, but after awhile, I was able to build a growing customer base. Once I realized there was a potential and I could actually make freelancing work, I decided to jump into the cold water and dedicate all of my time and energy to building my own business.

Working as a photographer has been a beautiful experience. My approach to this craft is very different from how press photography works. I really love people and having their trust to take their pictures (a very personal experience for many), so it's been incredibly rewarding. I get to spend time with different people and I can take the time to really see them. I'd probably get bored if I had a regular career path. I also wouldn't be able to look at people as deeply as I like to. I believe it's important to hone your own style. In the creative industries, you either get booked because you're cheap, or clients hire you because they admire your way of seeing things. At first, I was playing it safe like everyone in the industry, but there was this one specific assignment that completely changed how I approach my profession. I was hired to take people's portraits for a corporate website. I remember being tired of the neutral style, so I decided to try out something different. Retrospectively, I just didn't want to work with a hand flash anymore. Then, when they called me up afterwards, I felt slightly anxious when picking up, but hearing the excitement in their voices and their admiration for the images gave me the confidence boost I needed. I realized it was me who stood in my own way. If you build a strong voice, a recognizable style, people will come to you for exactly that!

How is your business set up?
A lot of my clients are companies. I work with big companies, but

then also small businesses. I get hired to take their employees' portraits, or to photograph the executive board. I also work with artists; I do test shootings for model agencies and I shoot for magazines. To me, it's important to stay true to my photographs. I really don't want to lie through the images I take. Naturally, my images might not be the usual, but I really believe I get booked for the images I capture.

I have about eight to ten clients I work with regularly. They make for about 70-80% of my income, and then I work on smaller, more spontaneous projects.

How would you describe your attitude towards travel?
I've never been a luxurious kind of traveler. During school, I'd go on trips just to see how life was in other countries. Back then, I'd go to Italy. Today, I might be able to explore Japan. Over time and with the money I earn, the further away I've been able to go.

Travel is a good reminder of how blessed we are living where we live. We tempt to forget that! We tempt to separate "us" from "them," but it's mostly because of our lack of knowledge. You often hear how dangerous various places are, but I've learned it's always the idea of them that's scary. We're only scared before we arrive somewhere. In 2008, I traveled to Australia with a stop in Taiwan. Everyone warned me that no one there could understand English and how I should be careful. I was nervous, but when I arrived, I was totally fine! Even if you don't speak the same language, you always have hands and feet and can somehow communicate if you try. People are friendly. Everyone was so helpful. I felt slightly crazy for letting others discourage me. The same happened with Sierra Leone. Everyone I told that I was going there was freaking out about me going there as a white, blonde female. And guess what? People there are just like you and me! Polite and nice!

Of course, sometimes people can be ugly. And it's not that there weren't any situations where I didn't feel scared. But I was always scared before I went on a trip. I'd book a flight thinking, "Wow, did I just really decide to go travel through Colombia for weeks by myself?" Once I arrived at the so-called dangerous destination, everyone was always really friendly. Colombia has been one of the most beautiful journeys I've had to this day.

I believe in the sharing economy. I keep my doors open to both friends and strangers and have people stay with me. Sometimes I stay with others. To me, an open house attitude really means a lot. Saving money isn't my first priority. It really is spending time with people I care about.

In every country I've traveled, it's always been easy to find people to share with. If you want to rent a car, you'll probably be able to find someone to split the costs with and share an adventure. It's easy, especially when you're easygoing yourself! Of course, sometimes different expectations might collide, but then open, honest communication can solve all issues. Talk, but also listen!

I usually only have a backpack when I go somewhere. It allows me to be flexible. I no longer book an accommodation way in advance. I'll take care of it once I land. Sometimes, I'm lucky and I have friends I can stay with, but then, mostly, once I make a trip out somewhere, I really want to explore and see as much of a country as possible. In Europe, I rely on carpooling or I'll take a bus or a train. In Asia, if there's someone who offers to give me a ride for $20, I might just do that if they feel trustworthy to me. I've gotten into enough cars in my life without knowing the driver. If you manage to handle the moment and listen to your guts closely, it can lead to some of the most incredible stories. I love that by being on my own when I go somewhere, I can allow for little serendipities to brighten up the days.

How did you start implementing travel into your work life after you went freelance?
Having worked independently since 2011, I now know the cycle of my business. I hardly ever receive any bookings in January and July. I remember my first year when I went on vacation until the

6th of January and expected to get back to a full inbox. I started getting nervous when, for the entire first half of January, no one reached out to me. I was close to calling people. However, February and March rolled around and I was as busy as ever! It really taught me a lesson to observe when the need for my work slows down and just go on vacation during those times. Like Easter. Easter's always good to take time off!

I have months when I work seven days a week because there's so much demand, and then again, there are times when it's pointless for me to hang around and hope for an assignment. For example, when I went on a vacation to Iceland for three weeks in July 2016, I only got one call, so I was more than happy to give that client contact details of another photographer.

What allows me to balance work and travel as I do is that I proactively call people several weeks before I leave and ask whether they have a project where they might need my services. My travel plans help me structure my business and be in full control of how many weeks a year I'm out of the country. I go somewhere at least four to six times each year, and I make sure two of these trips are at least three to four weeks long. Typically, I leave during my slow months, January and July, of course! To make sure I really take off, I only take my analog camera with me. It's then not just about traveling slowly; it's also a way for me to savor each image I take much more deeply. Shooting analog film is the ultimate luxury for me. I can allow myself to be in the moment and focus.

I almost never bring my laptop. Unless I want to take the time and write, but still, I prefer not to. I really like turning off my phone and not being available to anyone but myself and the nature I'm surrounded by. But it's not always easy. We're so used to being on all the time, it's become hard to take a step back. But then, I really think it's worth it! So for me, it's not just about implementing travel into my work life. It's also about allowing myself to disconnect and having the consciousness that I won't be missing out on anything. When I first started freelancing, I was really scared to go on a vacation. I was scared to lose a client or not to earn enough money once I got back. But now, years later, I know people hire you because they like working with you. The quality of my work and my attitude and relationships with my clients matter, and unless they need something urgently, I know they'll wait until I come back.

Of course, sometimes, there's a nice shooting I could have done, but I also know there will be many others in the future. Taking the time to explore other cultures is important to me, so I prioritize it!

How do you communicate to your clients you're not going to be available?

Over the years, I've built very loyal relationships with my clients. I work with the same companies regularly, so it's just about me telling them that I won't be available for appointments for a particular amount of time. I usually ask for appointments proactively.

The longer trips are hardly ever spontaneous. I know way in advance when I'm going to be out of the country just because I book flights and take care of my visas. That's why I inform my clients about two months in advance. While I usually tell them in person or call them to clarify when I'm not going to be available, I also always follow up with an email to make sure they receive the information in written form as well.

In case a client reaches out to me while I'm out of the country or busy with other appointments, I always refer someone to step in. What's personally important to me is to only refer people who put as much attention to detail as I do myself. Many creatives fear they might lose a client if they refer someone whose work they respect themselves, but I've realized that if that really happens, then the client's better off with the other photographer anyway! Usually, my clients stay with me and are grateful I made sure their assignment is being handled properly.

Being self-employed, how do you balance your work life?

First of all, I have a dog, so that gives each day structure. I must go out for a walk for at least 30 to 60 minutes. That's already very relaxing. Even though I love my profession, I'm hardly someone who puts work first. I might go swimming or play with my friend's kids. I'll have fun whenever possible, but I believe I also have a good sense when it's time for me to get back to work. Some days are just so much fun that I end up working late nights. And that's great too! My work isn't just client appointments. It's a lot of post production. I mostly try to work when I'm in the flow. And then, when I have deadlines, I simply must account for them.

Of course, during my busiest months, I'll have to get up and get out of the house earlier. Also, I exercise regularly because part of my job is to carry heavy equipment and I just know if I don't look after myself, I'd get exhausted much quicker.

While my workload varies throughout the year, I still try to have at least one day a week off, even during the busiest times! I keep a running list of places I want to visit; a small town somewhere close to Vienna, a lake, or a mountain someone tells me about. When I meet someone from a foreign country, or even a different county, I'll always ask them what they'd recommend for me to see in their area. I seek little adventures every day. Sometimes, I bring my dog, and other times, I ask friends to take care of him. I've built a good support network. I take care of my friends' dogs when they're on vacation and they take care of mine. I'm lucky because my dog is of a calm nature and people love to have him around, even though he's a Galgo, which isn't necessarily a small breed.

How does it work out financially for you?
I spend money as it comes. I'm usually not the best to talk about budgeting because I don't budget. I save €300 each month and I put the money in a separate account. It's an emergency fund for when the car breaks down, for my potential future plans in case I ever want to buy a house, or for travels if I go over budget.

I'm very aware of the seasons within my industry. I know the times when I'm likely to have more work than necessary and times when no one's going to call me. I've found peace with the fact that I won't probably ever have a stable income and earn the same each month.

When I travel, I try to find ways to work on project I might be able to monetize later on. Not that I'd focus on work fully, I just know I might be able to sell a story or some images here and there. I work with an agency for photographers. They negotiate with potential clients on my behalf. Sometimes, they might even sell some images from my backlog. That can even happen years after I've traveled somewhere. The photos never get old!

How do you budget for your travels?

Usually, I don't assume I'll spend much more when I travel abroad compared to how much I spend at home. What's different, of course, is that I don't earn money during my travels. I need to count for that. I tempt to stay with friends if somehow possible. That doesn't just save me money, but it's also a great opportunity to reconnect with someone you haven't seen in awhile.

It might be that because I've established myself as a photographer, I don't really look at my account as much. There are times I might run out of money or moments when I overstretch my budget, but I also know that I'll be able to earn it back in the future.

What's something you'd recommend to others who want to travel the way you do?

When you go somewhere, don't plan upfront. Instead, once you arrive, ask locals for recommendations. You might end up in places off the beaten path where not that many tourists visit. My partner and I once ended up going to a remote island because a local vendor told us it was his favorite place. It took us two days to get there, but it was totally worth it and it really only happened because we were open to it.

I'd also say you should be grateful and respectful at all times, and at least make the effort to say "hello," "please," and "thank you" in the local language. We're all just people and we're all trying to make the most of our lives. Be kind and friendly and help make life worth living for yourself and those around you!

Michèle Pauty on
Web: michelepauty.com
Instagram: @michelepauty

BECKY BURTON

IT'S OKAY TO
SHIFT YOUR
PRIORITIES
TO DO WHAT'S
IMPORTANT
TO YOU

What's been your educational and professional path?
I've always been enamored by different cultures, and, more importantly, how people from different cultures interact and relate to one another. I'm equally enamored by languages and how each one has a unique phonetic texture, as well as a unique way of narrating the world. Given these areas of interest, I double majored in International Studies and Linguistics during undergrad, and also got a certificate to teach English as a second language. That certificate allowed me to study abroad in France and teach for a year, while simultaneously learning French.

After graduating university, I worked for a few nonprofits and quickly realized I was more interested in empowering people to determine their own paths through economic gains than I was in providing direct services. In other words, I wanted to connect people and countries to opportunities to earn more, rather than build schools, roads, libraries, or other services. I believe that once people are empowered economically, they're able to decide the best development strategy within their cultural context.

This thinking led me to pursue a master's in Economic and Political Development, with a focus on Corporate Social Responsibility. Within one month of my two-year program, I knew I wanted to work at the intersection of applying business acumen to development and bring the case for "doing well by doing good" to business. Since earning my master's degree, I've had the immense privilege of working at that intersection, focusing primarily on environmental stewardship and sustainability in the corporate setting.

After working for a few years in the field, I also added a side business – a hobby, really – of creative writing. In late 2014, I published my first novel, which I describe as a 140-page love letter to New York.

How is your business set up?

For the purposes of this book, I think it's most helpful to describe how I combined creative writing with consulting – and padded income from both with savings – to be location independent for nearly two years.

First, to give a little context …

Just days after my mom edited my entire novel single-handedly (an incredible feat performed in under a week) my siblings and I received an email from my dad titled "Unhappy News." He explained that my mom's breast cancer, which had been treated through chemo and radiation the year prior, had metastasized to bone cancer. Though it hadn't spread to her vital organs, the cancer was found in her shoulders, ribs, hips, and neck. The line from his email that hit me the hardest was, "The simple truth is that bone cancer is terminal." I always wondered what it would be like to receive that kind of news. It was tumultuous and earth-shattering. I was attending an event when I received the email, and I rushed out between speakers to sob in the privacy of a back hallway. I called one sister immediately and then took the subway home to call my other siblings and my parents. We all spoke throughout the evening in a web of calls across the country that could've been traced like a phone company's network coverage. We were all trying to make sense of the news and find comfort in each other, but none of us had any real comfort to offer. The conversations were loving, but still tearful and draining. She was still there, with her zest for life and peace about her future. But that future, while uncertain in length, had been given a tragic certainty about its ending. I'd been considering a move from New York for several months before receiving news of my mom's prognosis. While I found great fulfillment in my work, my love-hate relationship with the city was becoming heavy. After receiving my dad's email, I knew the time was right to move and shift priorities. I decided to leave the city, which meant leaving my full-time job, and consciously dedicate the majority of my time to friends and family for a period. I knew I wanted to find a series of side jobs that I could work in 1–3 hour chunks. It was important to me to be able to take long breaks for lunches or afternoon card games with my parents. I also wanted work I could do from any-where so I could also spend time traveling to see friends. In 2015, a mix of travel and home life made sense because my mom remained healthy, vibrant, and active for most of that year. To support my-self during this period, I primarily used my savings, and I was also incredibly fortunate to move into a part-time consulting role for my company. For a bit of extra income, I began writing short pieces on forums, though most of my guest writing was unpaid. Finally, I rounded out my work by starting my second novel. Though this final endeavor has yet to yield income, this became my main focus for the first year.

In between extended periods at home, I visited 11 countries over a combined total of six months, with the dual purpose of seeing friends scattered across the globe and researching the theme of my novel: making home. I explored the concept through house tours, as well as philosophical conversations about how people defined home for themselves. One important note about this endeavor is that I actually wrote down the idea for the book *three years earlier* in a stream-of-consciousness journal writing exercise. When I was cleaning out my computer, just before my first international flight in 2015, I found a document titled "Ideas," with the date stamp of March 2012. It was a series of ruminations on money, love, and pur-pose, and among the mental meanderings was a thought about the possibility to pursue multiple passions in life: "One idea is to be a writer for *Apartment Therapy* and travel to showcase homes all over the world, combining my love for all things creative with my love for travel, and showing how we can incorporate the beautiful parts of other cultures' viewpoints into our lives." It was so affirming to find my previous self's dream on the very eve of my commencement to fulfilling it. Looking back, I believe taking time to write down some of my deepest wishes in 2012 allowed me to internalize them and bring them to life, albeit a few years later.

Based on this experience, I highly recommend taking time, perhaps once or twice a year, to do a freewrite of everything that's swirling in your mind. Put those dreams and wishes on paper, no matter how wild they might seem, because giving them voice is the first step to their actualization.

A final note on "my business set up" during this period: though pursuing a freelance career was the right path at this particular point in my life, I don't want to give the false impression that its "rightness" made it easy.

For one of the series of paid articles, for example, my story pitches were not accepted the first time. I submitted three options to the editor, but she told me none were a good fit for the audience. In a short response, she relayed this decision and recommended I get back in touch if I had more ideas. At first, I felt stung. I worked so hard on crafting creative ideas and felt like I really had a chance! I took a few weeks to read through other stories on their site and eventually came up with new pitches, which were accepted. The lesson? You've heard it 100 times, but I'll say it again. You have to keep trying. Don't let your ego or pride hold you back. You have to keep planting seeds and know that not all of them will lead to a harvest, but keep faith that some will.

How would you describe your attitude towards travel?

I want to begin answering this question by pulling back the curtain on a belief which I think some travelers have, but very few admit or recognize. This is the belief that travel is a zero-sum game. In other words, I get the sense that many seasoned travelers feel they have to keep certain destinations a secret, or other travelers will "mess them up." I think others believe that seeing fellow foreigners in a place somehow detracts from the place's authenticity, as though Paris – the most visited city in the world – becomes less remarkable as more tourists visit each year.

Early on in my travels, I realized I held these biases, and I quickly realized how silly they were. New York is still crazy, frenetic, endearing, exciting New York, even if tourism increases (and likely because tourism increases) every year. Picnicking on the great lawn near the Eiffel Tower is just as enchanting whether you're surrounded by Parisian teenagers or Japanese honeymooners.

The reason I bring this up is that I think we must be careful not to become self-righteous travelers – those who would never think of being seen with a camera around their neck or stepping foot inside a global fast food restaurant. It's important to question the belief that there's a correct way to travel, and instead embrace that there are so many right ways to see the world, just as there are so many right ways to live.

Now, stepping down from my soapbox to answer the question, I personally love to travel to visit friends and family. I'm happiest as a traveler seeing new places through my loved ones' eyes and understanding their day-to-day in a new context. There's an everyday-ness to this type of traveling that really appeals to me. It provides an excellent window into local life. I love walking down the streets, smelling fresh bread, listening to people around me talk about last night's date or tomorrow's soccer game. It helps shed light on the commonalities and the rich differences among us.

My favorite part of travel, no matter how it's done, is that it demands presence of you. I find most people step out of the virtual world and into the real one more readily during travel. In a new place, we must focus on whatever we're doing and whatever is in front of us. It's much harder to go on autopilot. One of the greatest gifts I received during my six months of travel was the ability to look for the novel and unique aspects of every place, even familiar places. The world is big and there are so many remarkable things to experience, even in the city you've known since birth.

How did you plan your trip and how did you manage to work on the road?

Given that I'd been toying with the idea of leaving New York for a few months before I received my mom's news, I had discussed a possible visit with several friends in late 2014. The timing was right to visit in 2015 because many of these friends had moved away for short stints, and if I was ever going to visit certain countries – like Morocco, Cameroon, China, Colombia, Turkey, or New Zealand – it made sense to do it while they were there. Other visits – to Jamaica, the United Kingdom, Sweden, Malaysia, and Laos – were driven by the desire to see home countries of friends I'd met in New York.

My itinerary was based on these friends' schedules and their ideal timing for a visit. It was definitely not an around-the-world trip, but an itinerary that covered enough miles to circle the globe three times over, with lots of zig zags and stops to see family and attend weddings in the United States throughout.

Besides mapping out my trip based on various people's schedules, I didn't spend much time preparing. I was incredibly fortunate to have a built-in travel guide and place to stay everywhere I went, given that the primary purpose was to see friends. The most important things I did to prepare were buy a good backpack, hone my skills for finding cheap flights, and make a list of all the visas I needed (which were Cameroon, China, and Laos, by the way).

That said, I certainly realize most people won't be able to simply rely on a friend for accommodation and guidance in a new city. As such, the lesson I can impart from this method of laidback travel is the joy of no expectations.

Normally, when I prepare for a trip, it's done with much deliberation and planning. I wonder about the weather and the food. I try to picture the cityscape and imagine how the people might be. In other words, I travel with a set of expectations and then wait to see how reality matches up to them.

During this trip, the constant movement left little time for expectations to form. It was even rare for me to think, "Tomorrow I'll be in a different country," on the eve before a flight. Traveling to a new country became more like taking the metro to a new subway stop. Yes, it took a moment to orient to the surroundings upon arrival, but each place didn't feel entirely foreign. A beautiful fluidity took over as the borders melted away. By entering each country without expectations, I relaxed into the joy of just being there. By staying aware of real reality rather than my idea of what it *should* be, I was less caught up in constant comparison.

Besides reconnecting with friends, the research for my book also took a substantial portion of time. I kept busy finding people who were willing to let me photograph their living spaces and do an interview on how they defined home. At first, I was trying to write a chapter a week based on these interactions, but I quickly realized writing a chapter takes 20-25 hours. If I kept to the strict schedule of a chapter each week, there wouldn't be enough time left for exploration and connection. After the second country, I let go of this self-imposed pressure to write at that pace. I realized I was robbing myself of incredible experiences during the moments I spent in front of the computer.

I actually had a talk with myself, reminding myself I didn't need to do everything at once, but could take the literal journey – and the journey of writing – step by step. Instead of writing while I was in the various countries, I took really good notes to inform my writing later. It was another important lesson in how priorities can shift and how that shifting creates the best result.

How did you organize moving away from New York?

I gave both my manager and landlord two months notice. For me, it was really important to give so much lead time as a way to show my respect for the opportunities they'd given me during my long séjour in the city. I also feel that giving this notice allowed me to successfully transition into a part-time consulting role for my company, which was key from a financially sustainable perspective. Though I love building a home and nesting, I've learned not to become too attached to things, as I've moved several times throughout my adult life. At the time I left, I had no intention of returning to New York, and I was lucky to find a new tenant who wanted to take my apartment fully furnished. On moving day, I mailed two boxes home and took three duffel bags on the plane. I believe the less attachment you have to things, the easier it is to enjoy new places. This allows the intangible qualities of a place to make it feel like home (the pungency of the spice market, the soft quality of morning light), and you don't need to rely on a place's physical properties to feel comfortable.

I really admire people who travel with everything in a small backpack. I once read about a fellow who didn't even use a backpack. He kept everything in the pockets of his cargo pants! These are the sorts of minimalist role models I have in terms of packing.

In our society, we often express our identity through job titles, so can you talk more about how your perspective shifted over time?
Many can't imagine quitting, or rather pausing, a career during their 30's, which are prime working years. However, really analyzing and setting new priorities helped me feel comfortable in stepping off the career train. While it's really scary to jump off when everyone else seems to be continuing on, I've learned that there's always another train coming down the track. You can get back on whenever the time is right. You may not pick it back up again exactly where you left off, but that's okay. To continue the metaphor, it's important to remember that you still have the same bags you left with – the same knowledge and skills – and those will still be useful, even if the final destination changes.

Quitting my job, leaving New York, and focusing the majority of my time on family and friends taught me how multi-faceted life can be. Life doesn't have to consist of three chapters. It doesn't have to be school, work for forty years, and retirement. We can choose to make our lives much more varied and flexible; school, work, family, back to work, nomadic for a year, back to school, work a bit more. There are endless possibilities for how your particular chapters might line up. We have the control over our lives to ensure they meet our specific needs at a given time. Life can look so many different ways; you don't have to climb the career ladder and live a career-driven life if it's not what fills you up. Taking nearly two years away helped me realize how wonderful it is to make family a priority. Most people take care of parents while in their golden years. In my case, the opportunity to be with my mom presented itself during my prime working years. I don't have an ounce of regret in making the decision to move home and be with her. In fact, I give gratitude daily for the opportunity.

How does it work out financially for you?

This is a great question, and one of the most important lessons I can impart. Ultimately, I really made all of this work financially by saving in previous years.

When I was 25, I started a savings account. I put in $200 a month for nearly three years, and then never touched it. By the time I was ready to leave full-time work at 34, this yielded nearly $10K. Additionally, I started saving for about six months before I left New York. I started saving because I felt a yearning to move from the city, though I didn't know when that would be.

People always ask how I took a year away, and it is really thanks to that 25-year-old self and that 33-year-old self. Both of them had the wisdom to save, and then my future self was able to take advantage of that wisdom. While I've spoken mostly about my travel thus far, this is a moment when it's important to speak about the remarkable gift these younger selves gave the present version of me. The opportunity to live with my parents during the final year of my mother's life was the most exquisite, tender, and uniquely extraordinary gift I could have ever received. It was filled with precious afternoons cuddling on the couch, evenings spent strolling arm in arm to watch the sunset, laughing about childhood stories, and asking her meaningful questions like, "What will you miss?"

(The moon peeking through our windows and lighting the night, listening to grandchildren's achievements, large and small, and playing games in friendly competition, soon forgetting who won, were a few of my favorites.) It's hard to sum up in a few sentences how life-affirming and remarkably heart-filling those months were, but I look back on them as some of the brightest and richest spots in the tapestry of my life. If you can save now, even $50 a month, do it. Do it with no purpose in mind because the purpose will reveal itself when you least expect it and you'll be so grateful for your own foresight.

There's always money to be made, and the money you're making should go towards your priorities. Once I decided that being with my mom and reconnecting with my friends was a top priority, I knew this was how I should spend my savings. You might sometimes question when it's the right time to touch those precious savings, and I'd say it's when you want to focus on something else besides your career. Then, you have to be comfortable with the fact that there are saving periods and spending periods in life. You don't always have to save up. When the opportunity is right, it's okay to spend what you've saved. Saving should be about allowing your future self to experience something extraordinary.

How do you budget for your travels?
I did my trip on a budget of $20,000. This was covered primarily through savings, but also through my consulting and freelance writing. My plane tickets were the biggest expenses because my route was not economical. (I didn't do an around-the world-ticket because I had to return to the United States a few times for weddings and to be with my family.) Of course, I also spent far less than most people on lodging because I stayed with friends in nearly every country, so everything evened out. Based on these factors, and the fact that I only traveled for 6 months, I think traveling for a year could easily be done with $20,000–$25,000. I met a couple abroad that had put away $40K and were traveling for at least

eight months together, longer if the money lasted. Depending on how aggressively you save, I think a year-long break from work is possible after 1–3 years of saving.

What's something you'd recommend to others who want to leave their corporate job to travel?

The biggest challenge will be overcoming fear, not just overcoming the fear of relaying your decision to your manager, but also overcoming fear in the first months after leaving. Early on, I dealt with so much fear. I remember landing in my hometown and my stomach tumbled. I thought, "How is this ever going to work? What have I done? Was this the biggest mistake I've ever made to leave a secure job and step into the unknown?" When the fear hits, you have to remember that you've left your job, but you haven't left your skills and knowledge behind. Those skills, and new ones you will hone, will make the next steps possible.

Also, I'd recommend leaving your position with as much notice as you can give. Take your team's needs into consideration as much as your own. Two weeks is standard, but giving a longer notice will leave your team in a much better position and demonstrate gratitude for all you've learned and gained by working there. This will help strengthen connections and ensure your leave with a sense of mutual respect. Your priorities have shifted, but they might shift again. The adventure and time away from a 9-to-5 world will be wonderful, but after a year, you might desire the stability of full-time work. As much as wanderlust might be hitting you now, the desire to work might hit you later too! Leave your job in a way that allows you to return to your field with grace and poise.

Becky Burton on
Web: gusmcallibaster.com
Instagram: @gusmcallibaster

Ready for some soul-searching?

· *What sort of projects and clients impact your self-worth and determine your identity?*

· *What sort of clients and projects do you want to be associated with?*

· *What parts of how you run your business do you enjoy?*

· *What is it that you really love about freelancing that you wouldn't be able to have if you were employed?*

- *What parts of your business do you hate and want to delegate to others?*

- *What will you do this year to work on your business? (Don't forget to set a timeline!)*

- *What skills do you want to acquire before the end of the year?*

- *How are you planning to promote yourself this year?*

ABOUT

PURPOSE

While in the first two parts of this book, we've talked about success and mindfulness, thought about defining a framework for your business, and considered how you wish to receive appreciation, in this part, I'd like to invite you to focus on the three "W" questions.

When I first started researching this book, I was afraid I might end up writing a superficial lifestyle book that teaches you how to be a digital nomad in ten steps, just as it's fashionable in all the listicles you can find online. I knew that writing about taking extended breaks, traveling, and going on vacation might be considered as pure luxury. But then, amongst the first interviewees I talked with was Becky. Listening to her story made me realize that I'd much rather make this book into a guide to show you different approaches to a self-directed, conscious lifestyle, while acknowledging the fact that you too might question what you're doing with your life and whether you're on the right track. Which, by now, you might have learned is good and normal. We all need to regularly reevaluate what we're doing with our lives.

In this chapter, I want to focus on the following questions. Questions that you might want to ask yourself regularly. Questions to help you acknowledge whether the track you're on is the right one for you right now:

- *Who are you serving with your work?*
- *Why are you doing the things you're doing?*
- *What cause are you addressing with your efforts?*

Whatever you do, you need to have an impact on something and/or someone with your work to feel content and acknowledge your efforts. You can decide how much time and energy you want to dedicate to certain causes.

You can build your entire business model around having a specific impact, or you can pause work to make time to get involved in a cause that's close to your heart. You might want to do some volunteering, or you might need to take care of someone who needs you by their side.

Having a purpose isn't just about giving to charity. Having a purpose is about finding your place in society and positively contributing to the success of your community, or the community of your choosing. How you choose your clients, what products you create, and who is supposed to pay for them impacts how purposeful you are with your efforts. You might, for example, want to offer financial support to those in need, or you might want to get involved hands-on instead and offer your time to an organization you care about.

Highlighting purpose as its own part in this book is a way for me to showcase the benefits of work and the notion that what you do all day isn't and shouldn't just be about how much money you're making.

I hope you're still enjoying yourself! Please drop me a line on Twitter or via email to tell me how you like the book if you find some time. My email is hello@mkanokova.com.

1 CHOOSE YOUR PEOPLE

———

One of the questions people seem to ask themselves very often is, "What do I want to do with my life?" It feels like such a big decision for us to make. Given how often it's the topic I end up discussing with my friends, I figured I should also address it in this book.

In my personal opinion, the question of what it is we want to do with our lives isn't the question we should torture ourselves with. It's way too hard, and it feels like no answer is good enough to balance the weight of it. Often, by trying to define what we're supposed to do with our lives, we're trying to live up to who we want to be, or maybe to who we think we are supposed to be. Only seeing the finish line makes us forget that it takes years of becoming something. It takes years or even decades of practice.

However, when we seek what purpose our lives have, it's not about what we do with our time or who we are (that's ego, not purpose), but it's much more about who the people are we want to serve with our efforts. If you ask yourself who do you want to serve with your work, it suddenly feels like a question that's much easier to have an answer than what it is we want to do to fill our days.

To some, the answer might be that they want their family members to benefit from their work. It might be just the earnings that matter in order for them to provide for their family with the standard of living, time, and attention they wish. To others, it might be about the children or the elderly in their community. Others might want to help communities overseas because they don't agree with the impact our actions in our local communities have on their lives.

When you know who the people are you want to serve with your work – which doesn't even have to be just one specific group, it can be multiple – it will be easier to decide how you want to allocate your time and your resources. Knowing who shall benefit from your work will automatically make it easier to decide what sort of work or volunteering activities you might want to pursue.

For example, you might want to help people who live in cities do more sports. Maybe you want to empower young girls and boys from underserved communities to believe in themselves. It might be that you want to help people enjoy their time with their pets more, or help small business owners boost their sales. Whatever it is, it will be much easier to figure out what will make you feel satisfied about your work if you have the clarity of who you want to serve and how you want to contribute to their lives. It also goes without saying that having this clarity will guide you to find ways to make a living with your work, as it will be easier to explain what it is you're trying to achieve and why.

When I first decided to write *This Year Will Be Different*, I only wanted to portray women in the book. The reason why I decided to only speak to women was because after being Somewhere.com's community manager, the company where I worked before going freelance, I was responsible for featuring community members on our blog. While I never had a problem finding men who'd speak to me about their careers, I had a really hard time finding women who were willing to speak up. It wasn't the only job where I faced that issue. It's why I've tried to call out women to talk about their work and help shed light on females as role models ever since. While I might switch focus at some point and dedicate my energy to something or someone else that's meaningful to me (as there are multiple causes I feel strongly about), for now, I'm conscious of dedicating my energy to highlighting and showcasing women. And as you might know, this is just one of the communities I've gotten involved with.

Who we decide to serve with our work doesn't have to be a fixed decision. We can change who we serve, but we can also mix up how we serve the people we care about. The times as they are now are in favor of people who are multi-passionate. They either want to do different things to serve one kind of community they feel connected to, or they want to pursue different things to spend time with different people throughout their days. In my opinion, it's perfectly fine to be a designer-slash-writer-slash-teacher, and it's also great when someone wants to be a videographer-slash-barista. Different activities allow us to gain different perspectives. In the spirit of perceiving our lives as a journey, taking on different activities to connect with different people is something we should embrace rather than avoid. Spending time in the local café and serving old ladies coffee and cake, or handing out soup in the local homeless shelter might not boost your bank account all that much, but it might provide you with different perspectives, which will distinguish you from others who work in your industry. As Mitch Albom wrote in his touching novel, *Tuesdays with Morrie*, "The way you get meaning into your life is to devote yourself to loving others, to serving your community around you, and devote yourself to creating something that gives you purpose and meaning."

2 MAKE SPACE
TO GROW

———

Between trying to make a living and serving the people you feel dedicated to, it might be hard to think of making space to grow. I've already mentioned how important it is to make time to work "on" your business. A big part of doing just that is taking the time to educate yourself, gain new perspectives, and learn new skills. Whether it's by exposing yourself to new circumstances and learning from people face-to-face, or by subscribing to one of the many learning platforms online, making the time to learn new skills won't just help you enhance your business, it will also help you grow as a person.

Once you decide what it is you want to learn, you can look for ways to gain those skills. Should you not know what you could learn to enhance your skills, it pays off to look at meetup.com and browse through the groups that meet in your local community to learn together. You can also look up the website of a community college in your neighborhood and see what classes you could sign up for, and then do so! You might want to go into more depth with what you already know the basics of, or you can start learning a skill from scratch. You can sign up for a writer's club and improve at storytelling, or you can go to drawing classes to practice your observation skills. You can sign up for a programming class or learn a new language. Making time and being willing to invest money in learning something new to stay on top of what's happening in your industry is crucial. If you're a solopreneur, you'll have to be the one to take care of making sure your skills evolve in the pace of your industry. A challenge might be finding the time to learn new skills. If you decide to participate in a group learning activity, you'll have to carve out time that suits others too. However, it's a wonderful way to meet new people or bond with a friend if you decide to bring them along. It might be much harder to carve out time to learn new skills from the comfort of your home. I, for example, never grasped how to find time to listen to podcasts, which seems like such a great resource to so many people around me. I'm not someone to just sit down and listen to something. I don't commute, and I literally can't listen and pay attention to what I'm listening to if I'm supposed to focus on something else simultaneously. One thing I know about myself is that I need to keep my hands busy at all times. For years, it seemed like there was no space in my life to listen to audiocasts until one day, I realized I can wash the dishes and combine it with listening to podcasts.

My conclusion is that you might want to think about what you already do that doesn't need your full attention, such as washing the dishes, that you could combine with learning something new. If you'd like to learn more about creating habits, I can recommend Gretchen Rubin's book, *Better than Before*.The main takeaway from Gretchen Rubin's book for me was that combining something you already do with something new makes it easier to create a habit. But then, to come back to my personal example, and given you're probably someone who has a dishwasher, you might need to find something else that allows you to combine two activities. I usually watch Skillshare classes every time I'm ironing. Or, if you don't iron or don't clean your home yourself, there might be something else you do that allows you to combine it with acquiring knowledge. Not everyone might find cleaning as grounding as I do, but I also watch a TED talk or a Creative Mornings talk during lunch whenever I work from home. These are all just to give you some ideas how you could find time for learning.

Now, listening to podcasts or participating in a class isn't necessarily what makes us grow. What makes us grow isn't the dedication to learning; it's our dedication to stepping out of our comfort zone. For many, and of course for all the ladies portrayed in this book, stepping out of a comfort zone is certainly literal. The easiest way to step out of your comfort zone is by leaving your familiar surroundings and moving away from the people who love us and look after us. Being out in the world with people we don't know and have no connection to so we become solely responsible for our own well-being helps raise our self-esteem and makes us grow as people.

You can either travel to follow your wanderlust, simply allowing yourself to learn by observing how others do things differently compared to what you're used to, or you can travel to join a project and volunteer somewhere for a couple of weeks or months. A really good company that focuses on connecting creatives with companies around the world to do short-term projects is Wanderbrief, founded by my friend, Mark van der Heijden. Wanderbrief is a platform where freelancers trade their creative services for experience at companies abroad. Another good way to enhance your craft and stay updated with what's happening in your industry is by attending conferences. Not only are they a great way to visit a new city for a couple of days, but you'll also be surrounded by people who might inspire you to step out of your comfort zone and restructure your business if you feel like that's something that's needed. At first, you might feel like conferences are an expensive outlay, so you should really think about who the people are you want to connect with. From my perspective, the major benefit of conferences aren't the talks; you can watch these online. The major benefit is that you're in a room with a bunch of people with similar interests who you could work with on something in the future. I'd suggest you should make attending at least one conference a year a part of your life as a freelancer. If you don't have time to travel or just aren't in a place to do so right now, or what you want to learn isn't something you can take in while you do something else, or you can't join a class, try to turn the task of learning into a project and set accountable goals and milestones. If you don't set milestones or a framework to feel the pressure to accomplish something, you might drop out easily. If you've read *My Creative (Side) Business*, you might remember reading about this in more depth. I'm curious to know what it is you'll decide to learn and what conference you'll attend this year!

3 CARE FOR WHAT MATTERS TO YOU

—

What do you want out of running a business? More flexibility? Location independence? Time to have a family? Time to travel? The ability to sleep in?

Have you found a way to pursue what you enjoy doing, making the impact you want to have while still being able to pay the bills? Does your work serve the people you want to serve? Do they recognize your efforts in the way you wish to receive acknowledgement? Does what you do fill you with satisfaction? Is there something you desire that you haven't found a way to pursue just yet? And if not, do you have the courage to change it?

The 21st century is the first time in history when adults with an income have choices with what they do with their time and money. It's the first time where many in their mid-twenties and early thirties don't have kids yet. The questions of what one's purpose is and why one cares are all the more present for millennials than it has been for any generation before.

As long as you don't focus on helping a child pursue their purpose, which then gives you and your life a purpose, you have to figure out for yourself what it is you care about and what it is you want to create. That causes pressure. It's what leads to the millions of articles about people trying to figure out what they want to do with their lives. However, if you think about who you want to serve with your work and why you want to help those people in particular, it might be easier to define what gives you contentment.

PICK A CAUSE!

How do you give back? How do you contribute to society? Giving in its purest sense is most often what gives us a sense of purpose. The more we're fond of who we're giving to, the more we're at peace with ourselves. Generally speaking. What you give and how much you give should be in the framework of what's possible for you. For some, it might be money; for others, it might be time. As we often live in our small bubble of privilege, it's hard to empathize with people who don't have such a safety net to fall back on.

The greatest privilege there is isn't necessarily money. As we all know, we sometimes have more of it, sometimes less. And even if we earn more than enough, we might still think it's not that much because our spendings, if not controlled, seem to always adjust to how much we're making. However, privilege – at least, in my opinion – is the personal, social network you've built for yourself that you've either had access to from birth, or managed to find a way to step into. Privilege is knowing there are people around you who support you, look after you, and look out for opportunities you might be interested in.

If you're thinking to yourself you don't have time or money to offer because you need to pay back your student loans, it's still not an excuse to not care. Student loans or not, one of the smallest gestures you can do to share the love is to mentor and help people by letting them access your network. Of course, some people might not even have access to you to ask for help in the first place, so it's on you to offer help gratuitously. Who you want to help and what cause you want to support might be the two questions you're likely to ask yourself first. You might not even be aware of many issues. We're often likely to support something we have personally experienced or have compassion for because we can emphasize. Is it children, the elderly, animals, nature conservancy, or something else that matters to you that you want to support?

There are millions of charities and organizations for every cause imaginable, so first consider whether you want to get involved with a cause locally, or if you'd like your money and/or time to go towards a cause somewhere else in the world. You can either help financially or carve out time weekly, monthly, or once a year to get involved more fully, something you'll read more about in the upcoming interviews for this part of the book.

One thing I believe that's important for you to get informed about is how your money or goods impact the community you donate to. Is a donation to a community somewhere abroad really a good choice, or are you destroying some sort of ecosystem with your pledge you might not be aware of? When I found out how the clothes we throw into charity boxes impact the textile industry in Africa, I was horrified! It's important to really inform yourself how the ecosystem and community operates that you're getting involved in. You can always read information online. Nevertheless, sometimes it makes more sense to support a cause you fully grasp and understand the social context of. You might want to bring up the question of how others are involved and give back the next time you're having coffee with fellow freelancers and entrepreneurs to gain some inspiration for what you could do. Or maybe, as always, inspire others to follow your lead! It's in your hands!

5 PRIORITIZE!
DON'T BE BUSY

One of the most significant traits of our time seems to be busyness. We're busy because of our own ambition, drive, and/or anxiety. It's often said that solitude is avoided by people because of the fear of what they might face in the absence of hustle. It's become normal to always do something. It's not uncommon to feel guilty when you're doing nothing. It almost feels strange to just sit without fumbling on your phone. People are proud to say they have commitments because it allows them to feel important. However, what you fill up your time with depends on your personal priorities.

One of my favorite thoughts on busyness is from Gavin Strange. He gave a talk at the 2016 Reasons conference in Brighton, and it was all about making time for creative pursuits and how we are "all time buddies." We all have 24 hours in a day, just like Einstein! Just like Angela Merkel. Even your biggest idol only has 24 hours to accomplish something each day. What makes these people stand out is they know how to prioritize what's important to them. They put their personal values first. They make space to grasp and live out their purpose. Looking at the people we admire – whoever that is for you – it becomes clear what we fill our time with is a choice. Most certainly, we should strive to use our time for activities we care about. If you listen to Derek Sivers' words, he says that either you say "hell yes" to things, or you say "no." If you don't care, say "no," but if you do, "Hell yes! Go for it, then!"

Time is the most treasurable resource. While you can always make more money, you can't make more time. If you were to die tomorrow, the money in your bank account won't matter; as long as you don't have children or others dependent on you, it's up to you what you do with your life. That sort of responsibility, given no one wants to waste their time or be judged to have wasted it, might feel overwhelming. Anxiety of being judged for what really matters to you and pursuing that might feel like rebellion. Like having to break out of an (invisible) cage. I guess this is why it might feel easier to pursue things that are socially accepted. Following your purpose and desires instead of what's desirable in the context of the society you live in might feel bold. Then again, as I've already said, what matters is who you want to serve with your work and what you want to learn on the way.

If you know what you want to do or who you want to serve but never seem to find time for it, I've learned that when you stop prioritizing people who don't prioritize you, it saves time and energy so you can focus on what's important to you. As painful as it is to let go, it's most certainly freeing. Not prioritizing those who don't want to be prioritized gives you time you can fill with creative work.

To summarize, being busy with the little things and the people we don't care for all that much allows us to avoid questioning our actual purpose. Figuring out our purpose, why we're here, and who we want to serve with our work can be damn hard. So is questioning the status quo and optimizing our inefficient processes. Instead of facing what we know could be done more efficiently, we tempt to do things the way we've always done them because that's the safe and comfortable choice. Taking the time to think through how we approach different activities and errands might slow us down at first, but will essentially pay off. It can give us time that we'd otherwise say we don't have. Which, of course, isn't necessarily true.

When I first started working on this book, I desired to talk to people who were bold enough to prioritize free time or another activity that didn't necessarily help them enhance their career. In my social trap, I felt that climbing up the career ladder seemed like the thing to do to feel important. I constantly questioned who benefited from my work. I wanted to serve the creative community, dedicate my time to creative pursuits, and spend time with the people I care about without ever using the sentence, "I'm busy." I didn't want to be the person who'd type something into my phone while someone's sitting at the table with me, just because this needs to be done ASAP.

"I'm busy" is the answer you might've heard many times when you've asked someone how they were. It might also be the answer you've given to people. The answer, however, most certainly lacks enthusiasm. It's an answer that doesn't share the excitement over what you're spending time on. Instead, it pushes who you're talking to into a corner, expecting pity and not additional ideas. Being busy has become an excuse and the self-serving justification to cancel on others at the last minute. Often, people don't commit to things fully, scouting for other opportunities they might find more appealing. It's become normal to cancel or come late without apologizing, completely neglecting the person planning something who actually cares about what they do. It's hurtful. I personally believe it's selfish to treat someone else's time and effort as if their time was less worthy than yours.

Life is too short to be busy. Life is too short to make busyness the answer. Life is too short to waste your time and others' by not being able to immediately evaluate whether something is within your priorities or not. Before you ever answer that you're busy when someone asks you how you are, you should share what you're working on or what your current priority is, and what excites you that prevents you from accepting a dinner invitation. If done with the right portion of enthusiasm, people won't be mad, but will support you. Be true to your values, prioritize, and communicate! Be there for the people who care about you. Do the things you want to be doing.

*T*he conscious quest for purpose and the willingness to dedicate life to serving others is what struck me when talking to Yana Gilbuena, Kayleigh Owen, and Jule Müller.

Yana, a traveling pop-up cook, has made bringing people in foreign neighborhoods together to introduce them to Filipino cuisine her life's purpose. She wants to dispel myths and prejudices, and make what might be considered "dangerous because it's foreign" tangible to people. Yana consciously gives up comfort to help create a more united world that's not scared of sharing. I love and admire that!

I equally admire Kayleigh's desire to no longer be just another cog in the advertising machine. It's what brought her on the road and into this book. The willingness to step out of one's comfort zone and career track to look for something more meaningful is special. Kayleigh's story isn't one about a seamless transition; an overnight success. It's a story full of ups and downs and the quest to find a new path in life. It's the determination to do better and to be better that I found so incredibly meaningful.

It's also what made me ask Jule, the editor-in-chief of imgegenteil.de, to speak to me about her business, her values, and how she sets priorities in her everyday life. If there's one thing that's significant about Jule, it's that she doesn't fear stepping up and taking on responsibility. She was one of the first to drop everything and welcome the newly-arrived Syrians with open arms when they came to Europe in masses in 2015. She went out of her way because she knew that she could make a difference in someone's life. And she did.

I hope that after reading the following three stories, you feel empowered to make a difference in someone's life and will recognize that it's your turn the next time the universe demands your help.

YANA GILBUENA

GIVE YOUR

JOURNEY

A PURPOSE

FIND THAT

SPECIAL

SPARK

What's been your educational and professional path?

I was born and raised in the Philippines. There, I studied Pre-Med Psychology because I thought I'd go on to med school. It's a cultural stereotype. However, in my third year at uni, I realized it wasn't for me. My mother said that given I wasn't going back to school, it was time for me to move to the US. At the time, I felt like it was a punishment because at the age of 20, she asked me to leave all of my friends behind. But for her, she knew it was easier for me to get a greencard if I immigrated as her child. She worked in the US since 1983 as a nurse, so that's why she had a citizenship. Not being 21 yet, I was considered a child in America, so legally it was a family reunion.

When I came to the US, I didn't know anyone. I didn't have a peer group, nor did I have any work experience because in the Philippines, your only job is to get an education; not like in the US where a lot of people have part-time jobs. And, as you sure know, unless you have work experience, you won't get any work experience. It's a vicious circle.

I started working at a local coffee shop as a barista and started looking for jobs that would have something to do with what I studied. I got a job as a behavior therapist for autistic children at a company that didn't require previous work experience because they wanted to train their employees themselves.

I was going through a really rough time. Retrospectively, I'd call it a depression. It really was difficult for me to uproot my life and leave my family and friends, so I went out all the time and I was squandering all my money on drinks.

Then, at 23, I had a major car accident. It was pretty much a wake up call because I realized I could've died. I had this revelation that I had nothing to show. Do you know what I mean? There was nothing significant I created.

After that, I went back to school to study architecture. I'm passionate about seeing how design influences our everyday lives. It might be something as subtle as the design of a tooth brush or even a cup that makes us feel a certain way. So, there you go, I thought studying architecture was the answer! But two years in, I realized it wasn't the answer for me and I dropped out.

I started working in the interior design industry from scratch. First, I was a kitchen and bath coordinator before getting promoted to a kitchen and bath designer, then later on becoming a furniture designer and eventually an interior designer for commercial and residential spaces. That was in 2008 and you know what happened; the financial crash overwhelmed us all! Suddenly, no one had money anymore and no one spent the money they had left on remodelling their homes. In reaction, thrift stores became very popular, so I worked at an antique hardware store and, for some reason, also in the jewelry industry in downtown LA. Imagine me with diamonds stuffed in my pockets, trying not to look suspicious as I was transporting them from A to B. It was such an adventure! I constantly felt anxious, so I quit that job too after, like, three weeks!

Then, an opportunity arose and after seven years, I was able to visit my family back in the Philippines. I could visit my grandma again! When I got back to LA, I didn't want to live there anymore. I quit my job with a two-month notice and moved to New York.

I didn't have a job prospect or an apartment. I just thought I'd figure it out once I got there. It's funny how the universe works in the sense of how it provides to us when we need something. Being in New York seemed like the life I wanted and things fell into place quite easily! I made a lot of great friends and it was much easier than when I had first moved to LA. I even got a couple of job offers. You know, it seemed easy and Brooklyn felt like home. Things were good.

Then, two and a half years later, I got laid off from my job. It happened during a time when I was already doing Filipino pop-up dinners. Losing my job forced me to make a decision; I could either get another job in the design industry or try myself out as a full-time pop-up cook and jump into a new industry I wasn't very familiar with. I consulted a friend, a New York restaurateur, for his opinion and he made a suggestion that there were 50 states in the US and 52 weeks. I could go and do a 50 states tour and pop-up with a dinner every week in another state. It sounded like a fun project and also very doable, something I could figure out. So, that was pretty much the start of what I'm doing now!

How is your business set up?

I was a contributor to a local Brooklyn blog and they kept assigning me food-related stories. Supper clubs were on the rise and I absolutely adored the idea! Writing these articles gave me a chance to talk to a lot of the hosts and to my surprise, they weren't trained chefs. One was a psychotherapist, and another one worked as a TV producer. I had this realization that they set up all these amazing events on the side just because they were passionate about food! No formal training necessary! They loved creating this particular experience and that was their motivation. I felt very inspired and saw a potential to put Filipino food out there.

Living in New York, a melting pot of so many different cultures, I struggled finding good Filipino food, so I took it upon myself to introduce Filipino cuisine to New Yorkers. I organized my first pop-up in March of 2013 and started hosting dinners quarterly. After I did three dinners in New York, I hosted one on the West Coast. That was when I got laid off. Again, the universe was calling! After having the idea of doing 50 pop-ups all across America, I started planning my route. I began contacting people and asking if they knew people in places, such as North Carolina, North Dakota, and Missouri. Given I didn't grow up in the US, I had no family ties, so I had to ask my friends and tap into their networks. Everyone was just so supportive and helpful and they would connect me to people as far as three degrees away from them. The project was so successful because my friends would say, "This is the daughter of a friend of my aunt who lives there and there!" and strangers opened their homes to me, giving me their time and their beds, even driving around and showing me the cities where they lived. It was truly magical! You often really just need to ask and share your ideas to get a little closer to fulfilling them. I was able to see all these different cities and because I didn't have any expectations, I could fall in love with them. Because I saw all these places, from Nova Scotia to New Mexico, with my own eyes instead of listening to people's stories. This tour gave me a chance to connect with people on a completely different level.

Over time, I've learned how to make these pop-ups work quickly, so let's say Monday is my travel day. Depending on what state I'm going to, it could be just a short ride away or it could also be as far as 17 or even 23 hours away. Then, on Tuesday, I'd go out and explore the city. I make sure to find a farmers market and also try to contact local farmers. I really believe that the market is the heart of a city. I take my time and look for an Asian store where I can buy frozen banana leaves. I check out local cafés and talk to restaurant vendors. I get to know the area and its people. I do my research and I network. Tuesday is pretty much when I start building my little city-wide network.

When planning pop-ups, I always try to be very conscious and respectful of the local food scene. I collaborate with restaurateurs who appreciate having something going on at their space on their day off. I don't want to take away business from people who are dependent on their income, so I don't hold my dinners during their busiest nights. Sundays and Mondays are usually good.

To me, what I do is a win-win because not only do I make new people aware of these restaurants, but I'm also presenting the potential for new and alternative business models. I know that what I do has inspired others who now host pop-ups themselves!

When I venture out to a new city, I try to find a place that has chairs and tables already. Occasionally, I find myself in a situation where I'll need to rent tables and borrow some seating, but I try to avoid it because that would exceed my budget. So far, people have been very generous with sharing their spaces and equipment with me. I work with what they've got and if they happen to only have two induction burners, I'll just adapt my menu accordingly. I'll figure out a plan to make it work. Trust me, you can make almost anything work!

Sometimes, I meet people who are willing to share their space with me on Twitter or Instagram. Other times, I google around to find more about the local food scene and check out restaurants, then I just email them and ask whether they'd be interested in hosting me. I often google local bloggers and skim through their feed to see where I need to go and what I need to see. Even in 2017, not a lot of people know what a pop-up is, so I still have to educate people. Thankfully, I have a lot of press to back up my story. I think because of all the stories published about the work I do, it no longer feels like a stranger is taking over their kitchen. When I was starting out, I admit, it was different. Some people would be really snooty and ask me things like where I went to culinary school. It was very hard for some to understand that I never worked in a restaurant besides my own. But, then again, other people would be amazed I make pop-ups work and they'd tell me I was living their dream. During my research days, I look into the destination I'm going to next. I try to connect to local press and bloggers to help spread the word about my next event. Because I don't know anyone in the cities, I often just ask them whether they could connect me to people in their area. Meeting so many people and meeting them through their generosity is what I enjoy most about the sort of work I do. Thursdays and Fridays are usually my days off. By that time, I hopefully have everything set up. If I haven't defined pretty much everything by Wednesday, I might feel a bit anxious, but I've also hosted dinners where I didn't know the location until the very same day. That's what's so great about a pop-up! It's very spontaneous and you should never make too many promises upfront in case you can't deliver on what you said you'd make. I always decide on the menu when I see what's available in each town.

Wherever I go, I try to really see each city. It's important to me to spend time with locals. I ask them to show me where and what they eat, where they go for a drink, and what they like about their cities; what's unique to them. I love that I've been able to build little micro families everywhere I go. You can read many things on Tripadvisor or Yelp, but nothing will give you such an authentic experience as hanging out with the locals.

To meet people, I use Couchsurfing a lot, I ask my friends whether they know someone, and sometimes, I even use Tinder. There's no way I'm going to date anyone through Tinder. Honestly! I'm in their area for about a week, but it's such an easy way to chat to someone local and ask them about the good places to hang out or the neighborhoods I should see.

When you bring something new, something different to a town, people tempt to be very receptive and they want to be a part of it because they know it's temporary. I'm very upfront about only staying there for a week and that gives people a sense of urgency. What I do is often something they've never been a part of before, and it's also unique because no pop-up is like another.

Because I've been to a couple of pop-up dinners myself before I started hosting, I knew prices can be anywhere between $35 and $275. My personal goal is to make these dinners accessible to people wherever they live while keeping it within reasonable means. I thought $50 was a good price for people from varying stages of life, and it would be worth spending the money if I gave people a unique experience. Plus, $50 also felt like a price I could ask for in Chicago,

Houston, Saint Louis, or anywhere else really. I use eatfeastly.com to collect the money from the attendees. I've been with EatFeastly since their launch. If someone in Europe wants to try something out like what I'm doing, eatwith.com is a good platform for it.

I prefer to avoid flying because I carry sharp knives and don't want to risk have them taken away. I mostly take the bus or the train, or sometimes, I'm able to catch a ride.

The beauty of Filipino food is that I don't have to worry about bringing plates or cutlery with me. We eat from banana leaves, which you can buy in any Asian or Latino shop. We also eat with our hands, which is another part of an unexpected experience for many who attend one of my dinners. So far, it only happened once that I couldn't get banana leaves, which was in North Dakota. There, we just used butcher paper and it was fine.

How would you describe your attitude towards travel?
For me, as long as I have a roof over my head, a bathroom, and a kitchen, I'm pretty much okay with anything. I can sleep on the floor or I can sleep on a couch. I don't really care. I'm very minimalist when it comes to travel. If getting from A to B means taking the cheapest bus, I'll do that. Traveling in luxury is simply not my priority. Of course, that sort of travel isn't for everyone. While I love crashing at other people's houses, others prefer Airbnbs or hotels. To me, I know I can only keep doing what I'm doing if I stay on a budget, so I'll take whatever is free.

My suitcase is actually quite heavy. It's about 44 pounds, even though I only have a very minimalist wardrobe. Everything I own is black, denim, or grey to make sure I can mix and match. I prefer to keep my looks simple, and I do exchange my wardrobe regularly. I donate my clothes to a local thrift store and then I get new things. If I donate five pieces, I get five new pieces. I also always try to adapt my wardrobe to wherever I'm going. I wouldn't bring my Birkenstocks to Portland, Maine. It's pointless. So I have a few suitcases with clothes at my friends' places all over the country.

When I first started organizing pop-ups, my first destination was Key West, Florida. I was really lucky because one of my friends from Brooklyn just moved there and was a bartender at a local restaurant. He helped me set it up and introduced me to a lot of his friends.

At the beginning, I had a documentarian and she stayed with me for 26 states before deciding to move onto other adventures. It's an utterly different experience when you travel by yourself because you don't have to make sure the other is okay. The first couple of times I did a pop-up in a different state, I was just focused on making it work. I didn't want any hitches happening and I always made sure to have the next city lined up. In a business such as mine, you're dependent on people's good will. They could change their mind any time, so you have to be flexible and be okay. Being open to rearranging and having a plan B, or even C, D, E, and F helps. With everything I do, there's a lot of navigating and working around. It's what keeps me on my toes. I always think of a backup for my backup plan, like renting an Airbnb if a restaurant drops out at the last minute, or if I can't rent an Airbnb, I need to ask someone to use their house or go to a public park.

When you look for solutions instead of problems, you can turn any misfortune into a positive experience. The first couple of times, I was very rigid, but I've learned you have to work with what you have within your means. Whining doesn't bring you anywhere. It might be more work to cook on two induction plates instead of four or six, but it's still doable. It might be a challenge, but it might make the event far more special.

How do you explain to people what you do and that you're only there for a limited period of time?
I try to tell my story as simply as possible. I tell people that I travel and I cook Filipino food. I explain what it means to do a pop-up dinner, and I educate people about Filipino cuisine because most people think it equals fertilized duck eggs or even dogs. Where they

get that from, I don't know! I also tell people why I'm doing what I'm doing. I let them know that I'm very passionate about introducing people to our cuisine and our culture, and I believe food is the best medium. To me, Filipino food is like a beautiful tapestry with a lot of different influences because of our history. It's a little bit Spanish, a little bit Chinese, and you'll taste a bit of Mali or Indian. Filipino food might even remind you of some Arabic countries. I really want to show to people how diverse Filipino cuisine is.

Being on the road so much, how do you balance your work and your personal life?

I really appreciate the sense of freedom I have. I travel to different places, but then I can always come back in six months if I feel like it. I'm in no rush. I'm on nobody's schedule but mine, so if I want to stay somewhere for two weeks, I will. I don't have an apartment or a boyfriend to go back to, which, of course, is also a challenge. Keeping relationships and not having a place I call home is something I sometimes struggle with. I remember during the 50 states tour, I questioned myself heavily. I was like, "I'm here, sleeping in this person's basement on a futon. What exactly am I doing?" Sometimes, I craved going back to my own apartment in Brooklyn, having my own place and meeting friends for brunch. I missed seeing my friends, but then I would remember why I'm doing what I'm doing, why it's important to me. That keeps me focused.

While some people might have expected I would stop traveling around after my 50 states tour, the opposite happened. I knew that this was something I really wanted to do! After popping up in all the 50 states of the US, I went on a tour through the provinces of Canada, then I traveled to Mexico, and now I want to explore South America and Europe.

Sometimes, things don't go the way you want them to, and these are the times you miss having familiar faces around you. There's only so much you can talk about with strangers. However, through the work I've been doing, I've also been expanding my family, a wonderful support network wherever I go. Now, when I go to Bismarck, North Dakota, I know exactly who to call!

It's beautiful to create an opportunity to meet people and share a little part of my culture and myself with them. I love being a recipient of people's generosity and kindness. You don't see that as much anymore in this world. You know, I'm a stranger and I show up at your door and then you invite me into your house. We both know it will be fun! It's very unique!

How does it work out financially for you?

I make enough to be able to stay on the road and buy the things I need. I'd definitely say that I do pop-up dinners to be able to do more pop-up dinners because each one I host pays for the next. However, I also save. Besides my laptop and camera, I don't own anything luxurious, so from every dinner I host, I put at least $100 or maybe even $200 aside. I don't keep the money in my bank account; I keep it in cash. I know that if I saw it in my bank account, I'd spend it.

Recently, I've also started investing in a loft space in LA because I'd like to host dinners there, and I also have plans to host dinners outside of the US. From my experience in Mexico, I know that I'll probably be spending more money than earning.

How do you budget for your travels?

I know that if I only spend a certain percentage on food, I can still make enough money to cover my travel expenses. I like hosting a minimum of twenty people, but I've also cooked for a party of 150. I've also had dinners where only four people showed up, which happened in North Dakota. There might then be dinners with 75 or 90 attendees. It evens out!

The way I look at it is that I try to be minimalistic and get around as cheap as I can. At the beginning, I was very strict with myself and always tried to cook six courses, but now if I see that doesn't work out with the budget, I might do five or four courses, or even three!

I look at what groceries are available in each area and I stay flexible. I get whatever they have that fits my budget, and then I make my menu on the spot based on the season. I no longer say there must be an oyster dish or promise a menu in advance. Because, guess what? Oysters might not even be in season! I know that if I keep my spendings in check, I'll be fine!

What's something you'd recommend to others who want to travel the way you do?
Have a good purpose and assure yourself about why you're doing what you're doing. Find that spark that makes you want to get up every morning. It will make your journey more purposeful and more enjoyable.

Yana Gilbuena on
Web: saloseries.com
Instagram: @saloseries

KAYLEIGH OWEN

THINK ABOUT
HOW YOU WANT TO
CONTRIBUTE TO
THIS WORLD

What's been your educational and professional path?

What I studied has literally nothing to do with what I've been doing professionally! I studied International Politics. I was passionate about African development and learning more about different regions. However, I realized early on that most of my peers were hopping off to do something incredibly administrative in the political field, which definitely isn't my cup of tea. The thought of a bureaucratic job is still a massive no no.

I got very lucky because one of my good friends started their own company when I was in my final year, so right after graduation, I started working with her in a bootstrapped fashion ecommerce business. My friend is an extraordinary entrepreneurial character. I've always felt inspired by different women with a big vision, personality, and entrepreneurial attitude. I felt I could learn a lot from her, which I did. It was a great opportunity to gain insight into guerilla marketing tactics and the world of business when you have no funding.

Working in a startup has taught me that instead of sitting around and waiting for things to happen, you need to reach out to people and seek opportunities. I learned the "art" of cold calling people. We spent days calling people up. We'd guess people's email addresses and then email everyone, from HR to the CEO. I even learned how to knock on doors of creative agencies. We'd just scour the streets of East London. We always said we were graduates and would ask for 30 minutes of their time; it worked with companies, such as Yahoo, Net-A-Porter, or BBH, which I think is pretty good! I really learned that putting yourself out there can bring you to the best places.

However, my friend's fashion startup went into liquidation and I worked for a couple of small marketing agencies. I found out about The Body Shop grad scheme, but I missed the deadline, so in true startup fashion, I bought a coconut body butter, scooped out the butter, rebranded the packaging, and left a note inside. I sent it to the brand director of The Body Shop directly and followed up with a call to ask the receptionist if she could make sure it made it to the right desk. Shortly after, I was called for an interview and started the grad scheme the following September.

Then, after that, I worked for a Korean ad agency. The idea of a permanent job in one place, doing the same thing every day just didn't sit too great with me, and I decided to go freelance. I can't say I've stayed too long at any of the jobs I had. As a freelancer, I work as an account manager on a project to project basis. I step in whenever a company needs someone. It's not the easiest of jobs because no one hires freelancers when times are easy. I usually get hired because the company's overwhelmed with their workload and they urgently need more people to tackle the job. Along the way though, I've worked on some fantastically creative projects and met some of the most wonderful people you could meet.

At the end of 2014, I realized I needed a longer break. I wanted to take a step back from the hustle and bustle of London and get the hell off the hamster wheel. I needed to dedicate time to gaining new perspectives. It was time to really think about my next few steps before I got sucked into the next advertising job.

I knew I wanted to help women in some capacity. I have a fascination for Africa because it's so utterly different from everything we're used to in Europe. Knowing what my next direction should be, I reconnected with a friend who worked for a lodge and sustainable social enterprise in Malawi. I told her I was planning to travel and I was looking for charities to volunteer with. I wasn't interested in earning money; I just wanted to see how people work and learn how I could get involved. While the whole purpose of the trip was to see how different people around the world lived, I didn't want it to be completely soulless, so I tried to strike a balance. Of course, you can go to Thailand and just sit on the beach, which I've done a ton of times, but to me, it doesn't seem valuable. I wanted to be a little more hands-on. My idea was to help charities with their communications, their websites, and maybe even do a bit of marketing for them. I really think you don't need to be an engineer to help! Any sort of skills are useful and are most likely needed somewhere.

My friend referred me to a small design studio that was employing single moms and other women that became outcasts by the local community in Malawi and needed some extra help. It was a small project that only took a couple of weeks, but having a date I was supposed to be there made me make the move and step out of my comfort zone. I immediately booked a trip to Malawi!

I traveled to Kenya, Ethiopia, Zambia, Zanzibar, Thailand, Cambodia, Vietnam, Indonesia, Malaysia, Australia, US, and Canada. I did a few small projects here and there remotely for friends back in the UK to get paid, I worked on three different charity projects, and then at a gorgeous boutique branding agency in Melbourne for a couple of months. I enjoyed being in Australia, but I also knew it wasn't getting me closer to where I wanted to be long-term: working for a women's charity.

How is your business set up?

I usually freelance for a company full-time for a limited period of time. I work very closely with recruiters, who (by now) know what sort of environments I perform in best. They usually call me up when an opportunity arises that would suit my needs and ask if I'm available. It's taken a few years to get into this position. Initially, I worked hard on developing solid relationships with recruiters by being in constant contact and working hard on projects I took on. I've also developed a good network of people in the industry who often call me for jobs too. The way one finds good positions in creative agencies in the UK is through recruiters and industry connections. Having the job market being dominated by recruiters is not as common in other markets. However, if you're considering coming to the UK, that's where I'd start.

I remember hearing someone talk about recruiters being valuable, so I just went home and googled "best recruiter London." As basic as this sounds, it led me to a website of some sort of an award ceremony for recruiters. I looked through the list and reached out to a few of them. That's how I started getting better temporary jobs. Recruiters in the UK have good connections to the leading agencies and corporate companies, and their job is to source for top talent. The system works to my advantage because I don't need to commit to a permanent role, and as a freelancer, I can also ask for more money. The system is great because it allows me to work on a variety of projects and nip in and out of projects whenever I feel like it. More and more recruiters also cater to remote companies. If your connection doesn't, it's still possible they have other valuable connections. Many top recruiters have connections to smaller offices in other markets, so once you establish a good relationship with your local recruiters, you can ask for referrals when you feel like working in Australia, South America, or Asia. Many countries offer a working holiday visa if you're under a certain age, and you should make use of it before it's too late!

When I was on the road in 2015 and 2016, I kept in touch with the recruiters I usually work with. I believe it's important to keep them in the loop and let them know what I'm up to.

How would you describe your attitude towards travel?
Be mindful - in the original sense of the word. Be mindful of the local people and culture, and mindful of their perception of you. I think it's so important to have enriching experiences that travel offers without being exploitative. Traveling in the developing world is different from traveling elsewhere in so many ways. When travel-

ing around East Africa, I was much more aware of simple things, like taking pictures. I was fully aware of the kind of pictures I took and the language I used when talking about my experiences there. I don't want to perpetuate the same old narrative about struggle and poverty in Africa; one we're constantly fed. Of course, that's a huge part of the African story, but there's so much more, which is why I always endeavored to get a local perspective on things and share that side of the story before making a judgement.

I like experiencing a culture first-hand. I like to get involved and be helpful. I don't plan much; in fact, I plan very little. I only make a list of places and things I definitely want to experience and make sure I do that. Overall, I tend to let everything else fall into place. Of course, this isn't always smooth and can be tiring when you're constantly planning on the go, but it's a more natural and exciting way to travel (within a budget) and it's easier when you're on your own.

How did you plan for your big break away from freelancing in the UK?

I knew I wanted to go to East Africa. I'd never been! My friend was there, so I knew I could have my base at her place and then take outside trips. It's not that I did much planning. I planned my starting point and I knew that I'd be running out of money after about six months. I planned to go to Asia and then onto Australia and stay there on a work and travel visa before flying to Canada where I had to attend a wedding. Regarding work, I asked friends and locals if they knew of any local charities, or I searched online beforehand. I tried to avoid big, clunky charities. There are so many small but fantastic Facebook groups dedicated to volunteering that you can find just about anywhere. It's definitely worth checking out.

I booked my outgoing ticket and planned a few checkpoints for the next couple of months. However, I also made sure not to have too many plans because you might need to change your mind on the go. And often. You might meet new people and do something else than you've originally planned.

How do you communicate to your clients you're only there temporarily?

Given that most of my contracts are negotiated by a recruiter, it's very clear from the beginning that I'm a temporary employee. However, I always make sure that people know I'm a hard worker and won't let them down or ever leave anything unfinished. I'm there to do a good job!

Before my contract ends, I always have a meeting where we discuss if and how we will continue working together. I'm non-committal. I commit to the period of time we both agree on, and then I leave if I have to or stay if there's more work and I like the organization.

Workplaces are generally flexible. If you're good at what you do, they'll always try to meet you halfway. A lot of people think that companies want to squeeze the most out of you, but they really don't. They're by far not as rigid as everybody always assumes. I think it's a case of just communicating what you want and taking it from there.

Another thing I should mention here: I never fall out of touch with people. It's natural for me to send an email here and there just to ask how they're doing. You can stay in touch via email, LinkedIn, or even Facebook. Even if I take a break, it's important to still stay in touch with people back home because you'll want to return to something one day. It takes time and it requires you to be organized, but find a way to be just that! Make the effort!

When you travel, you'll have a feeling of uncertainty. You won't know if you get a job immediately upon your return. You probably won't know at all what will happen when you get back, so having strong relationships will help you not feel utterly unrooted when you get back home after several months of being on the road.

The way you treat freelancing, do you separate between working for money and enjoying pleasure and fun projects?

Yes. I hope to one day find myself at a point where I only do what I really want to be doing, but now I'm still transitioning. However, I also think it's important to constantly try new things to learn and grow professionally and personally.

Around your late twenties, many start getting married, buying houses, and having kids. It's something I eventually want as well, but right now, I'm on my own journey. I know how I want to contribute to the world and I'm seeking a way to do just that.

Traveling by myself has been self-affirming and very empowering. It's a good feeling to be in charge of your own life, your own choices.

How does it work out financially for you?

I freelance, which is how I save up. As a contractor, you earn more money than in permanent positions. When you plan to travel, there's a lot of pressure and people telling you that you need a budget and a plan. Certainly, you need some savings. But if I were to save at a normal pace, I might have lost interest by the time I had enough money saved to be able to hit the road. I estimated I should save about £8,000 before I would be able to leave London.

I had a big goal and knew I needed to make sacrifices to be able to hit the road within six months. First of all, I took on a job that I might've been less excited about, but paid more. Then, I moved into a place where I paid less rent. I walked to work every day instead of taking the subway. I stopped eating out and instead of buying my super expensive cosmetics, I'd fetch the house brands whenever I ran out of something. If some shoes or something broke, I wouldn't have gone to the most expensive store to replace them, but looked for a good deal instead. I had a figure in my head. I wanted to save £1,000 for each month I was planning to be on the road, and maybe some extra cushion if I needed an overdraft. I knew I could also always pick up work on the road if I needed to.

One of my biggest motivations during that time was a girl I worked with. She was always going on long vacations. She'd mention in our conversations how she put £600 aside this past month and I kept thinking to myself that if she could do it, I could too! It was really good having a friend who was doing something similar and earning roughly the same. Seeing her save up so rapidly motivated me to, for example, pack my own lunch in order to save some pounds.

People really underestimate how much one can save on these little things, like lunches, travel costs, cosmetics, and so on. Often, money is about keeping up appearances with the people you're surrounded by. From time to time, you must acknowledge that some experiences are worth throwing money at and that saving up might take longer. But even when you then travel, once you notice you might be broke soon, you can pick up a short-term project remotely. In the meantime, and I'm sorry to say, saving up makes you less social. Being social is expensive. You'll need to remind yourself of your big goal regularly!

How do you budget for your travels?
Before I left Britain, I only did a basic research. I looked into *Lonely Planet* and some local blogs and forums. I talked to a couple of people who went to Malawi and asked about their experiences. That helped me learn more about what sort of accommodation to book or what kind of transportation is generally considered safe.

When you're from Europe, certain things seem so self-evident and we might forget that just because we can catch the bus in front of our doors, it might not be the safest option for a woman traveling by herself in Africa. All these extra spendings are things you need to consider when setting your budget. With the actual budget I made, I think it took me an hour to gather the data I used for it. I didn't make an excel sheet or anything. I just jotted down notes on a piece of paper to get a better idea of how much money I should have. I worked out a daily average. I looked into how much a room would cost me. For example, in Malawi, I knew it was about £18. Then, I thought about how much I'd be likely to pay for food, which I figured was about £7 to £10. I then put a pound or two extra on top of each day and I multiplied the number by the days I was planning to stay. Then, of course, you'll end up having expensive and cheap days. If you do it for each country, you'll get to a number that you'll have to put aside before you leave.

When I was becoming broke in Africa, I knew I had to leave soon. It's not a cheap continent if you're a tourist. You end up having many expenses you wouldn't even think of back home. Suddenly, you need private drivers to get from A to B. That stretches your spendings significantly.

In Asia, I needed a bit less money, and by the time I got to Australia, I was really broke. I knew I had to find work quickly. I might've had just under £1,000, which is something like £2,000 AUD, about enough to lay down a deposit for a room. I remember I landed and went straight to the Melbourne library, took out my laptop, and started researching agencies in the area. I updated my LinkedIn profile and approached people I thought might know someone who could help me find a job. It's all very obvious steps, but we often forget to put them into practice. Once again, I was hired through a recruiter. I started working within maybe 10 days after my arrival.

What's something you'd recommend to others who want to travel the way you do?
Commit to it. Whatever it is you're thinking about doing, set a date, book a flight, and hand in your notice. Whatever it is you need to do, do it! I was talking so much about leaving, but I only started saving up once I booked a flight and made it clear to myself that it was truly happening.

Kayleigh Owen on
Web: bit.ly/KayleighOnLinkedIn
Instagram: @po_kay_

JULE MÜLLER

CARE!

FOR YOURSELF

AND FOR

OTHERS!

What's been your educational and professional path?

I wasn't really sure what I wanted to do after high school. I started studying Fashion Design, but I wasn't necessarily good at it. Afterwards, I tried out different things before landing a job at Universal Music Publishing where I worked with songwriters signed to the company. I then went to London for four years to work as a community manager for both Channel 4 and an international gaming company. Social media was becoming a thing then, and because I've always had an affinity for the online world, it felt like I found my sweet spot.

After moving back to Germany, I started working for an agency as a conceptionist. While working for the agency, I sometimes worked on freelance photo assignments, such as weddings. While working there, my best friend, Annelie, and I had a project idea. We came up with a concept for an an online dating site and called it *im gegenteil* to feature singles in their homes. It started out as a small passion project. I struggled finding a boyfriend and none of the options available, given I'm an introvert, seemed suitable for me, so we felt something like *im gegenteil* was missing.

When we researched the concept we had in mind, we couldn't believe that no one, not in Germany, Britain, or even the US, had the idea to portray singles in their rooms, so we launched the site in November 2013 without making much noise. We wanted to see if people were interested. The timing was pure luck because around the same time, Tinder launched in Germany and they brought the whole topic of online dating into the media. Journalists loved the comparison of Tinder, the fast dating, and *im gegenteil*, the slow dating counterpart. It gave us a lot of free press. We didn't know how we'd be making money with the website, but we saw the growing interest and it felt right to take the plunge and try to make something bigger out of it. We both quit our jobs to focus on *im gegenteil* full-time.

Annelie and I were both really excited about the opportunity. We knew we could make ends meet and live off of our savings for a while. I was also offered a book contract around that time, and while I didn't think I'd publish my first book about my confused twenties, having the advance was what enabled me to go without a job for a while.

How is your business set up?
When we first launched, we didn't have a business plan. When we decided to work on *im gegenteil* full-time, we had no idea how we'd make money with it. Honestly, I must say earning money was a topic we avoided talking about for a long time. It had been planned as a side project, and thus, there was no real structure to how we managed our time. We worked constantly. I checked my emails every couple of minutes. I didn't eat or sleep regularly.

One day, we visited a personal finance coach to portray him for our online magazine and he picked up on something Annelie and I said to one another. He pointed out we had an unhealthy relationship to money and he wanted to help us out by offering us a coaching session. We thought he'd teach us how to use excel sheets and how to map out a business plan, but instead, he talked to us about our personal relationship to money. I used to think that having money meant I must be an evil person because only evil people were rich. I needed to get rid of that mindset. Annelie had some personal issues regarding money herself. Doing the coaching as a couple was great because in the weeks following the workshop, we'd remind the other whenever we noticed we were falling back into our patterns. When we first launched our site, the subtitle of *im gegenteil* was "Singles in Berlin." We never dared to dream about portraying people in other cities, not to mention in other countries. Over time, we've learned to look beyond our immediate horizon. The business coaching has made us much more confident. We're now able to recognize the value of our work. We learned to acknowledge that we've created a great platform, and collaborating with us is worth something. Of course, we had to figure out how to include advertising in our work without making *im gegenteil* too commercial. We didn't want to place products in people's apartments because that would have felt sneaky. Authenticity is really important to us! We decided to instead collaborate with brands that would give us their products for raffles, or we'd go to places and events and portray people there. We've also made ourselves available to brands as content creators. While we didn't earn any money in the first year, we had a much better second year, and after three years, we can afford a comfortable life.

Before I became self-employed, I always felt I was working too much and that I never earned an appropriate salary. However, since Annelie and I have our own company, we no longer have that feeling. We're fortunate to be spending our days in a fulfilling way, doing what we enjoy.

How did you restructure your business after the coaching session?
We used to believe that one must work hard in order to deserve the money one earns. We were proven wrong because it's more about being smart about how one works and not how much one works. We were constantly hustling. We'd either work out of my place or Annelie's, or sometimes, we'd work at a local café. We worked for hours and hours. Days and nights.

I hadn't really been on vacation for three years. It's clear that at some point, you become uninspired. We had an opportunity to move into a coworking space for content creators, the Blogfabrik, and once we moved in and found a community, it became much easier for us to get new ideas and work in a much more focused way. Now when I'm at home, it's no longer work. It's become easier for me to relax.

In a second series of coachings, we worked on our personal and business visions, the actual direction we wanted to head in. Sometimes, it's easy to lose your focus when you're tied up in your daily work too much, so it's important to compare thoughts on where you're heading with your business partner because your views may change over time.

Setting goals, priorities, and values for the company is incredibly helpful. If you don't know where you want to go, you'll end up somewhere, but this might not be the place you actually want to be. It's a simple and obvious advice, but still very powerful. Bringing everything to paper was a long process, but it's helped us a lot.

In 2015, you took long breaks to help the newly-arrived Syrians. How did you juggle all your volunteer activities and your day job?
It wasn't planned that I'd take time out to volunteer. It simply happened. My flatmate collected some money and asked me if I'd like to join her to drop off donations. You can't just show up there with stuff you think they need, so we headed to LAGeSo, the initial processing point for asylum-seeking refugees in Berlin, and asked what was in demand. When we got there, we weren't prepared for what we found. Hundreds of men, women, and children were waiting for help. The situation was out of hand and we knew we had to stay and get involved directly. It was out of the question not to show up the next day! We were there at 8am. And I kept coming back day after day. It was clear I couldn't sit at my laptop and write blog posts about dating while all these people who didn't speak our language, nor understand our system, needed help!

After two weeks, Annelie and I decided to announce a summer break on *im gegenteil*. Instead of heading to the beach, we headed to LAGeSo. We knew it was important to show others what was happening, so we kept updating our social media channels and

I also put together a manual to explain how people could get involved themselves.

After a month of working at the site, I was incredibly exhausted. My body couldn't take it anymore and I got sick. None of the volunteers were trained to give emotional support, so it was of no surprise my body was filled with adrenaline 24/7. I've learned that asking for help is essential, so I started seeking for someone who could give me supervision, a type of counselling given to professionals engaged in working with people in a mentally challenging way.

After the session, I decided to become more focused with my help and instead of trying to help everyone, I tried to help four young men. My flatmate and I invited them to stay in our apartment. I was very intentional about offering my help to young men because they were the last to be given help by the official entities. Most men who arrived in Germany slept in parks or on the streets. It was devastating to see our governmental support system failing us!

At the beginning, I paid for all the expenses of the boys I invited to become my family. Once I noticed how impossible it was to finance food, tickets for public transportation, and other bits and pieces for the five of us, I asked my Facebook friends for help. Within a couple of days, I had more than €3,000 in my bank account. Everyone was really supportive!

While *im gegenteil* is an online magazine about dating, we decided the refugee situation was just as, if not more, relevant in that moment. I wrote about my experiences and tried to activate as many people as possible to help. It was important to give the refugees names and show them as people, not as anonymous masses that stormed into our country as it had been portrayed in the mainstream media.

I still do hands-on volunteer work. I have, for example, joined a project where a group of young adults crowdfunded a ship, IUVENTA, to conduct sea rescue on the Mediterranean sea. I also went out to sea for a couple of weeks myself, which was a tough but incredibly rewarding experience. I now use my online reach to help projects like this that need donations.

How do you communicate to the people you work with that you won't be available?

Annelie and I have been best friends since 2004. We're so close that we don't need to talk much, so when something is important to one of us, the other one notices quickly. What has really impressed me was that Annelie assured me if I wanted to work in development aid and quit *im gegenteil*, she'd understand. It's important one doesn't take work-related things personally.

While my full-time engagement was temporary, I dropped out of my job quite unexpectedly. If Annelie would've said she didn't want me to volunteer, I might've had to reconsider my choices. She knew how much *im gegenteil* mattered to me, but also how much it mattered to me to help when it was most needed.

Annelie is good at other things than myself, and while she deals with the client-facing side of our business, press, and marketing, I'm the one who mostly takes care of the content and visuals. When I go on vacation, I usually try to prepare everything that's needed in the upcoming weeks, but sometimes things aren't ideal. That's usually also when you notice all the not-so-obvious things your business partner does in their day-to-day. Showing appreciation and being empathetic is crucial to ensure good team work.

How did you start implementing breaks into your work life?

I had jobs that kept me on the road during my twenties and I used to do a lot of backpacking. Now, a vacation in a remote house in Brandenburg suddenly sounds just as appealing to me as going to a remote island! I started doing yoga and have become more aware and mindful of my mental well-being. Sundays are always my days off and I don't touch my laptop. I've also started choosing destinations where I won't have such easy Internet access. Being as addicted to the internet as I am, it's good to try to control my compulsive use. Annelie and I have both noticed how beneficial it is to take time off. We don't just go somewhere for extended weekends; we also make sure to hang out at the beach or travel up north and enjoy the fresh winds of the Baltic Sea for two weeks at a time, and do so more often throughout the year.

How does it work out financially for you?
I've never worried about not having money. I know that I can always get a job in a store or at a bar. Naturally, I want to have work that fulfills me, but if I need to put groceries in my fridge, there are other possibilities for me to do so. My mother taught me that you can always try something out, and if it doesn't work, you can try something else. I live by that.

Building a company takes time and it was our conscious decision to build *im gegenteil* together. Each of us owns 50% of the company and thus, 50% of the profits. We've been focused on building our business, and it's been worth it to both of us to use our savings to be able to do so. Sure, it would be nice to think about pension funds and all the other investments one is supposed to think about once one turns thirty. However, sometimes you need to invest your resources in achieving the goals you have defined for yourself. I really enjoy my day-to-day. I enjoy the work I do. That makes money secondary.

How do you budget for your travels?
Given I take money out from my bank account when I need it, it's not necessarily that I'd spend much time on budgeting. Even when I take time off, I still don't go overboard. I stay within my means.

What's something you'd recommend to others who want to engage in charity work?
I believe it's become obvious to most of us that one can't just close their eyes and not face the injustice in this world thinking it will go away. In my opinion, we must all do something to help preserve

our community and environment. Whatever the cause is you decide to help out with, exploitation of the poor and the weak, social grievances, political abuse, wars, environmental degradation, or animal welfare, there's enough to do for all of us. I used to have millions of excuses why I'd never get involved. I used to say things like, "I don't know anything about the situation," "I don't have time for this," or "I don't know anyone there." Getting started is the hardest because it's about jumping into unknown waters. However, the good news is there are already enough people in the world who do good and you can just approach one of them and ask how you can get involved.

There are also millions of ways how you can contribute with your skills. You can collect money, donate money, help organize, and explain what you've learned about a cause to others. You can plant a tree, hold someone's hand, or just invite your new Syrian neighbor over for a coffee and show them they're welcome.

In other words, look for a cause you care about, research what organizations are out there, grab some cookies, and go talk to them. You can start today; at least with the research!

Jule Müller on
Web: julemueller.com
Instagram: @jule_mueller

You're not going to ask yourself what you want to do with your life here, but...

· *Who are the people you want to benefit from your work?*

· *What cause(s) do you care about and why?*

· *What can you do that will contribute to the well-being of your local community?*

· *What is it you will do this year that will help you grow?*

- *What is it you need to do to boost your self-confidence and tackle issues that make you feel uncomfortable about yourself?*

- *What's something that could happen that might make you feel like you've failed?*

- *What's something that's out of your comfort zone, but you're curious about and promise to try before the end of the year?*

ABOUT
4 MONEY

*I*f you've been following my writing, then you know I'm not a fan of "one size fits all" solutions. I worship the notion that everyone has their own strategy to how they deal with changes and personal challenges. In my texts, I want to give space to diverse opinions and let you decide what applies to you, what you can draw from.

Writing a book about freelancing would most certainly feel incomplete, had I left out money as a subject. To me, it was important that with each and every interview you get to read in this book, you don't just learn about the individual ideas of what it means to lead a fulfilled, self-directed life; you also learn about the financial side of things.

I've never had the desire to interview the rich and famous, even though everyone I spoke to for all three guides has the potential to become just that. And yes, all the women I've ever showcased are most certainly recognized and what I'd consider successful. They all know how to support themselves with what they love doing.

My aim with writing and publishing these guides has always been to tell stories that feel relatable to wherever you may be in your life. I aim to highlight different possibilities and to use them to give you a little nudge so that you dare to reach higher. I want you to feel confident enough to do so because you've learned from their insights and strategies.

Money and our relationship to it is personal. Everyone has a different idea of how much money is necessary to pay for their everyday expenses, as well as how much one needs saved up to feel at ease should things not go as planned.

We all have specific ideas for how much we believe is reasonable to pay for rent; whether we buy our groceries at the organic market or at a discounter. It's up to us to decide what it's worth for us to spend money on. Do we eat out regularly? Spend our income on cocktails? Do we shop for clothes? Furnish our apartment? Go travel?

Each of us has an idea of what makes for a good life, and everyone's idea of what a good life is might be different and possibly not comparable. At the end of the day, everyone should make enough and possibly more to finance their own version of a comfortable life.

On the following pages, I'll try to shed some more light on earning, saving, budgeting, and investing money. Don't consider me an expert. Just like everyone else, I have my habits, my shortcomings, and most certainly, a lot of catching up to do on proper financial investing.

As you've already seen, I've asked everyone I interviewed for this book how their businesses work, how they feel about money, and how they budget. Consider this chapter a summary of what you've already read with some additional thoughts from my personal experiences.

1OWN IT

———

So, how much money do you really need per month? Have you ever thought about tracking your expenses?

When I applied for a master's program, I knew I'd need €10,000 to pay the student fees. I didn't expect to have much time to work during that time, as it was a one year program. I figured I should get a loan that would cover the tuition fees, but also my everyday expenses for that year. To be able to calculate how much I needed, I had to figure out how much I was spending and what expenses I could potentially reduce in case I needed to. I needed to set a budget before filing an application for a loan, so I started tracking my expenses.

Once you start being meticulous about your spendings, it's close to impossible not to have that overview of your funds. Tracking your spendings helps you feel in control. The reason I'm mentioning this here is for you to know how I deal with my money. I track it. Religiously. So before I go on, you should know awareness is my secret to stability.

I pay all invoices I receive immediately. I send out invoices the minute I've finalized an assignment. In most cases, but definitely once an invoice is over €1,000, I ask for a 50% downpayment before I start working on a project. I charge my clients rates that are high enough to cover all the emailing back and forth, and I'm also the person who will send you a reminder that you haven't paid yet. And I will do so exactly two weeks after I send out an invoice. I track my business expenditures with Freshbooks every couple of days, and I prepare my receipts for my tax advisor at the end of each month. That takes about 30 minutes. I don't allow for things to pile up. I know how much I need to earn in a year. I'm fully transparent with my tax advisor about my plans and my values, which enables them to consult me in a way that I can make the most out of my business. Every year, two months before the financial year is over, I ask my tax advisor to calculate my future payments for taxes and health insurance based on what I've earned already and what I know I will earn before the tax year ends. Thus, I know what invoices I must expect to pay in the future and by when. If an unexpected bill comes up or if I made a mistake, I no longer panic. I think to myself I'll just have to work more to make up for it; that's pretty much the biggest change for me, given that before and while I still had a fixed work contract, unexpected bills would've knocked me over completely. At the end of the day, I had a loan to pay off! I don't say my system is perfect. But it works pretty well, and I believe it will be easier for you to retrace or disregard what you read in this part of the book if you know how I approach the financial side of running my business.

As you all know, the one thing that changes when you decide to go freelance compared to working for a company is that you give up your regular paycheck; the paycheck that covers your fixed costs and everyday expenses. The paycheck you know will be there, even when you have a rough month. I guess it's the one thing all freelancers and creative entrepreneurs have in common; their monthly income is hardly ever the same. There are months where money comes in easily and months where not a single penny rolls in your bank account, unless you pay yourself a salary, something Liz does whose story you'll read at the end of this book.

If you've read *My Creative (Side) Business*, you know I've been pushing the idea of dedicating time to producing products with the aim of building additional income streams. My theory that I laid out in #MCFSB was that there are a lot of companies looking for creative content, which they can then produce and/or sell to then pay you in royalties. Royalties aren't a way to earn money fast. But it's really comforting to know that on specific days each month, you'll get a paycheck and this paycheck will keep coming for as long as your products keep selling.

Now, getting back to your earnings, or more specifically, how much you need to earn. If you have a number of how much you need to come around, multiply that figure by two to get the amount you must make before taxes. That's the minimum you need to earn to keep afloat and that's what's good enough for the beginning. I know there's a hype around having a six-figure income, and while that's admirable, it's definitely not the norm for the majority. It's also not desirable if the quality of life and the mental space to enjoy the little moments are being overruled by having money as the sole focus of your life. They say money isn't what makes you happy for a reason. That cup of coffee with your best friend, your partner, or your kid might!

In my theory, and over time, if you keep building your reputation, if you keep putting out your best work, and keep invoicing people properly, you'll be good. If you remain focused on building your roy-alty-based income streams, you'll be better. #SMARTCREATIVES, the hashtag I've been using, came around for a reason. If you focus on building your portfolio of work and your scalable income streams, you'll be able to boost your income without increasing the time you dedicate to work. And that's something, I believe, is worth working towards in the long run. I hope you agree!

2 FILL UP YOUR PIGGY BANK

One of the most valuable books I've ever read about personal finance was Alexa von Tobel's *Financially Fearless*. It's a book targeted at women who want to pay back their debts quickly. My main takeaway from her book was that you should apply the 50/20/30 rule to how you manage your income.

According to Alexa, you should budget 50% for your essentials: rent or mortgage, utilities, transportation, and groceries. Budget 30% to cover your lifestyle and do so guilt-free: eating out, shopping, entertainment, personal care, and of course, travel. The remaining 20% of your income should go towards your future. It's the money you should keep for emergencies and retirement savings, to pay off debt, and to save up for a home if a home is something you wish to own.

I like the idea of budgeting money, and kudos to everyone who's so organized to remain within the suggested framework. Given money management for freelancers is an act of constant juggling, sometimes it might make sense to cut down costs in the essentials and the lifestyle departments in order to save up for whatever you have planned for your future, or whatever you've treated yourself to that needs paying off. There are millions of strategies that people have established to save money. A technique that might work for some might not work for others. You might be someone who's okay with keeping their desires in check, or you might be someone who prefers to go out and then work more. Or, you might not have a choice, as you might be trying to bootstrap a business or have other responsibilities that need be taken care of.

There are multiple perspectives on saving money, and while we've gotten pretty far into this book without bullet points, I've decided to illustrate bullet points here if I want this chapter to make more sense. Here are some of my thoughts and observations of possibilities to fill up your piggy bank(s).

Earn more than what you can spend
The most logical way to save more money is by earning more than what you need per month. The less you need or the better your royalty-based income is doing, the easier it will be to follow this strategy.

Pay yourself a salary
Decide what you consider a suitable salary to cover your costs and pay yourself a fixed amount each month on a specific day. This strategy works much better if you have separate bank accounts: one for your business and one for your personal expenses.

Rethink where and how you live
Keeping your spendings in check and rethinking what you spend your money on is definitely worth it if you want to put more money aside than you currently do. To me, the most pragmatic way to save up without sacrificing your lifestyle is by keeping your fixed costs low. The less you pay for rent and utilities, the more you can make out of your life without having to sacrifice your personal freedom. I believe the easiest way to save is by sharing an apartment with others, downsizing to a smaller room or a flat if you don't want to live with others, or moving to a neighborhood or town where rent is more affordable. It might often be that if someone travels a lot, they're clever about how much rent they pay and how they monetize whatever they own.

Reduce and eliminate all that you don't need
If you live in a small space, you'll have to reduce your stuff, which reduces your spendings. There's no better way to reduce the amount you spend on possessions than by reducing the amount of storage

space you have. Think of all those large cupboards and closets; once you have them, you'll find a way to fill them too. Eliminating the amount of storage space in your apartment will help you downsize your possessions overall!

Don't buy things immediately. Reserve, then come back!
One of my favorite tricks to control what I spend my money on has been the speed in which I buy things. When I see something I like, I ask the cashier to have it reserved for two days, and if it still possesses my mind after a day, then I go back and buy it. However, sometimes even with the strongest will, things can happen. I'll never forget how I left Marrakesh with three carpets in my luggage, even though I only intended to buy one. In my defense, Moroccan salesmen are exceptionally good at their craft...and you can always sell things if they're worth buying, which brings me to the next point.

If you buy things, buy assets
It's okay to spend money on things you can either make money with or you can sell at a higher price than what you've paid for. That's then called an investment. If you're in no place to buy and resell property, try vintage furniture or Lego. It's a pretty good investment from what I've learned. And yes, I can tell you the Lego story over a glass of wine, should you fancy to hear it...

Give your savings account a purpose
It might be easier for you to put money aside if you know what you're saving up for. It might be even easier if you give yourself a deadline for when you want to have saved up that amount. Keep a reminder of your goal on your computer desktop, next to your desk, in your journal, or your wallet. Make it visible to yourself what it is you're saving up for.

Pay everything cash only
So, I never quite understood how people pull this one off, but a popular trick is to make it very visible how much you have at your disposal by pay-

ing everything in cash. In countries where cash isn't an option, there's an app to solve that dilemma. It's called Wallets. Once you commit to this strategy, keep tight. Really try not to spend more than how much you carry around with you. Phew!

Plan ahead and make detailed budgets
If you need to be more aggressive about your savings strategy, then make budgets for how much you're willing to spend on each category. Once you have a figure, try to reverse-engineer how to stay within your allowance. Think about how often you can go out for food, have drinks with friends, go to the cinema, what sort of products you buy in the supermarket, etc.

Establish shopping routines
Take one afternoon and think about what sort of recipes you cook and what sort of groceries you buy. Whether you can come up with new recipes that are made out of cheaper ingredients or rethink where you get your groceries from, there are ways to save up on food without sacrificing its quality. I've learned that if I buy vegetables at a farmers market, it's much cheaper than at the supermarket. I don't know how that is in other countries, but it definitely applies to my local market in Vienna.

Don't shop online. Ever.
It's just too easy to curl up on the sofa on a Sunday night and order some things that look great on Instagram. Do me a favor; just don't. It's much easier not to do something at all than to do something a little bit.

Know your guilty pleasures
And put these on a budget. Don't eliminate them completely. You're a human, not a robot, but give yourself a cap of how much it's okay for you to spend on this treat per month. If you tempt to buy too many magazines, only get one or two a month. If you're a sucker for going

to concerts or seeing indie movies, think about another activity you could compensate this activity with.

Get a savings buddy

Do you have a friend who's also trying to save up for something? Turn your ability to save into a competition, just like Kayleigh did.

And once again, get a good tax advisor

They understand which of your overall expenses are business expenses. They know what things are tax deductible, which you might haven't even thought of. See your tax consultant as your ally; be open with them about how you run your business and what's important to you. They will help you save money you didn't even think you had! And, from my experience, don't be scared to shop around until you find a tax advisor you feel comfortable talking to openly.

You might not want to try and implement all of these strategies at once. One at a time is enough. Try out one strategy each month to develop a proper financial plan over time. The only thing I'll say again is that the more conscious you are of your finances, the easier it will be to put money aside to then pay for bigger plans, such as a year-long vacation, a secondary education, acquiring bigger investment assets, or maybe to finance some of your bigger personal plans.

3 BUDGET YOUR TIME AND MONEY

———

You don't just make budgets for how you'll spend your money. You also make budgets for how you'll spend your time, and most importantly, what you'll fill that time with. It's your choice whether you decide to take on a few high-paying clients, or whether you want and need dozens or hundreds of people to buy your products to contribute to your income. You decide how many hours you'll dedicate to volunteering or community work, if any at all, and you also decide how many weeks (or months) a year you want to take a vacation or travel.

You might have an ideal of how many hours you want to work, and by now, you also probably know how much you need to earn to be able to afford the lifestyle you wish to have; how much is enough for you to have your desired lifestyle. Taking all of that into account, you'll get to a number of hours you have per week, per month, or in a year to get to that figure.

It's logical, but also often forgotten, that not everything you could do pays the same. Some of the skills you have might pay much better than others. Some products you create might make up a bigger share of your earnings. Figuring out what products and services are easy for you to offer that pay what you want is your personal challenge and a part of the everyday freelancing game.

As is saying "no." If you agree to everything that comes your way, be it assignments you don't feel are the right fit or favors you'd much rather not do, you're being dismissive of the time you need to go after the assignments you personally care about. Saying "no" is part of budgeting time for projects you actually want to work on. It's as simple as that! The more projects you focus on that you care about, the more of such project proposals will land in your inbox.

Generally speaking, the more proactive you are about what you offer and to whom, the more people will notice the work you do. Specifying what you offer will also help you make your outreach more focused, and finding leads might become much easier.

One of the approaches to freelancing – and scaling without hiring – is something called productized services. It's not the same as producing content to sell via third party services, which is what I described in #MCFSB. A productized service is a systematized service that's supported by tools and has highly automated processes. They're generally easier to sell because communicating what you offer is no longer about who you are as a person and how it is to work with you, but rather about the benefits and the outcome you deliver.

Productized services have a price tag that's public, so the people who come to you are already almost onboard because they came looking for your kind of solution. By the time they approach you, they're familiar with the conditions and are close to making the final buying decision. You're likely to save yourself a lot of negotiating.

In the most ideal case, productizing services allow you to decouple the time you spend on the production and maintenance of a service from the benefit for the client. And even if not, it might at least save you a lot of your coordination efforts.

One big part of freelancing is onboarding clients, emailing them or talking to them on the phone. From my experience, onboarding clients might sometimes get out of hand and distract you from doing the actual work. I believe all your project management time needs to be covered by your remuneration. But then, I also think you should give thought to how much coordinating you care to do overall and choose your clients based on that. Some clients are (as you probably already know) high touch, and you need to enjoy these interactions or find ways to automate, systemize, or outsource this part of your business in one way or another. Generally speaking, outsourcing and automation, not just regarding your client work, but how you run your business in general, doesn't happen overnight. Finding ways to opti- mize a business takes time, which is why we so often postpone dealing with it. If you consider outsourcing as an option, you must consciously make time to rethink your processes and make them more transpar- ent for someone else to take over. (And yes, I'm working on a plan- ner for freelancers to help you tackle all that.) For now, what are the tasks you do in your day-to-day that you'd like to eliminate? And are there solutions that would allow you to automate certain processes or outsource them?

Why don't you think about what annoys you for a second, and then consult Google for what you could do about it? And then do it!

I hope figuring out just one thing today will make you feel like it's been a good day! Now, coffee!

4 INVEST YOUR MONEY, OR AT LEAST YOUR TIME

―

At 29, I had the sudden urge to figure out my personal finances. I felt like it was part of being an adult and I finally faced the fact that I had no idea. Around that time, my bank sent me a letter announcing they were reducing the interest on my savings account to 0,002% (not even making a joke here). Given the yearly inflation, I realized one was losing money by having money.

Right.

It's funny when you learn what your parents thought was a good idea to do with money in order for it to grow isn't such a good idea after all. For the rich, hamstering money on a bank account probably never was a good idea anyway. Go figure...but then, what do you do when financial literacy has never been part of your upbringing? That you don't know much, if anything at all.

As you can imagine, once I started researching the subject matter, I felt more confused than ever. I read *Rich Dad, Poor Dad*. I started learning more about personal finance and what options you can have when it comes to investing money. I still feel I'm very much at the beginning of understanding finances. Also, I only just paid my student loan back. As you can see, I'm most certainly not the right person to give you any sort of advice on this subject. However, one thing that I can share from my two years researching this subject is that before you have money to invest, you have time to invest. You have time to invest in yourself, in your projects, in your name, and in your reputation.

I'm not the right person to help you figure out your financial invest-ments. However, I think I'm in a position to say this: invest in yourself. Do something that will make building up that initial fund easier for you in the long run. Do something now. Play and experiment and allocate money for it so you aren't sad in case you lose it. Tim Ferriss, a role model to many young entrepreneurs, did just that. He called his fund of $120,000 his *Real World MBA*, and he was willing to lose that money in the span of two years as long as he learned more than he would have if he went back to school. To me, $120,000 feels very far away, but I like the idea of having a fund for the sole purpose of experiment-ing; a fund that's guilt-free play money with no other purpose than to learn. Yep, you're the boss now!

LEARN TO PRIORITIZE

In this book, you've read about all sorts of aspects surrounding money. You've read about saving money, spending money, and even a little about investing money. Given I've already written two other books about freelancing, I tried to keep this part as novel as possible. For #WTART, I've mostly asked questions regarding budgeting and all the different kinds of funds people have. I was most interested in how much different people put into their different funds in order for them to feel safe to then take off and see the world freely.

Feeling safe is the keyword. Money is what gives us safety, so it's common that money is what makes or breaks our courage. Sometimes, it's not even our own perception of money, but rather how the people close to us feel about our decisions and their financial impact. Our safety. Often, they might discourage us from the decisions that are closer to our hearts. Possibly because they're afraid it won't be safe, or because your decision in one way or another jeopardizes their own rank of priorities.

It's of little surprise that courage is directly related to how we're doing financially and how important money is to us in general. If we know money doesn't matter, we're much more likely to make decisions freely because we know that even if things go wrong, we'll be okay. If there's no money, we're much more likely to take the safe route, whatever we consider the safe route to be.

When thinking of financial stability, I consider it the ultimate goal to be in a place where you can make decisions freely from their impact on your lifestyle. To me, having enough money to be able to rely on my self-confidence and then take chances as they come is what I strive for. I want to be able to make decisions that aren't safe, but daring. Decisions that allow for learning and growth.

My personal strategy has always been to keep my fixed costs low, buy things I can resell easily, and only buy what I know I really need. I don't sacrifice on lifestyle: going out for food, drinks, and having coffee with friends. I buy all my clothes in black or grey as to not exchange my wardrobe regularly, and when I travel, I don't go overboard either. I spend my money on what's important to me; I don't waste it on things that aren't. Paul Jarvis once said that all the money you don't spend is all the money you don't need to earn. He's right, so I simply keep my spendings in check. I try to earn more in a month than what I spend, even in those months when I'm paying for flights or extra accommodation.

When interviewing for this book, I asked everyone how they budget. I also asked everyone about their safety cushion and how much they want to have on the side for them to pursue the sort of daring decisions that made me want to interview them in the first place.

I asked everyone about money because I knew money is important. I knew that money might be why you might dismiss certain ideas as unrealistic. And I knew I'd like to address money before I address travel, the final part of this book.

I wrote this book because I was curious about how people took time off. One of the key learnings for me has been that the ability to travel the world doesn't correlate with one's earnings, with being rich. The ability to travel and enjoy time off has to do with one's awareness of how much is enough, prioritizing what's truly important, then dismissing everything that isn't.

While prioritizing sometimes means that you must skip things you'd usually buy, it also means you have to get rid of what you believe others expect from you. What should matter to you are your own goals, not the goals of other people.

Money is a tool. No more. No less. Money is a tool to enable you to have the life you want. It should be the life you're living now, not the life you imagine you might have in the future that you can only reach through suffering.

Take your wishes seriously and figure out how to get to where you want to be. However, allow for it to take time. Try to find a way that's enjoyable. And most importantly, give yourself permission to spend your earned money on the things you care about, on the things YOU think matter.

*G*iven money can often serve as an excuse to do or not to do certain things, I wanted to introduce you to three ladies whose thoughts shaped how I approached the part about finances in this book. Laura Karasinski, Yasmine Åkermark, and Natalie Howard all have very different lifestyles, and each of them has a very different relationship to money. What they have in common, however, is that they never prioritize money over time for self-care.

Laura, an art directrice, talked to me about consciously deciding how much is enough for her. How much she needs. She set a cap to how much she desires to earn to not let money and work rule her personal freedom. She loves what she does and people notice. Her work is stunning and she's in high demand. Setting a cap to her earnings through providing design as service is how she makes sure not to expend herself.

Some might disagree with that approach and say you must make a lot of money to be able to travel the world. Yasmine's story demonstrates that's not necessarily the case. Long-term travel is accessible and might be cheaper. Mostly because what you spend your money on changes compared to how you might be spending your money while living in your hometown. Additionally, Yasmine barters a lot. She even founded a platform to make bartering easier for others: Tibba!

If, however, you have loans, you might find all these arguments laughable. Well, Natalie might just prove you wrong. She's recently moved to New Zealand to get the kick of exploring the world while paying back her six-figure student loan. Instead of saving up, Natalie is a master of finding ways to monetize what she has. She has a five-year plan to how she wants to pay back her loan and her strategy includes things such as sponsored Instagram stories or Patreon. There's a lot to learn from her clever money making tactics. On a side note, you'll notice that I talked to Natalie while she was still living in the US.

Fingers crossed the following interviews will inspire you and give you some additional ideas to manage your finances right.

LAURA
KARASINSKI

MONEY IS
SECONDARY

BE NICE TO PEOPLE AND LOOK
AFTER YOUR HEALTH

What's been your educational and professional path?
I've always been a graffiti aficionado. But instead of going out to spray paint, I sketched in a book and collected everything that inspired me. I was a shy kid growing up. I struggled making friends. I spent a lot of time drawing instead of socializing. The internet has been a blessing because it enabled me to connect to people through my work. When I was 16, a friend asked me to design a tattoo. That was my very first paid assignment. I got €50 and I framed the bank statement afterwards. It made me very proud.

Someone suggested I should make a Facebook page for my designs. It sounded like a good idea, however, I was too self-conscious to use my name. I named the page "housemaedchen" and started posting pictures of my graphics, and over the next few months, people from all over the world started following along. They liked the images. They left comments.

Showing my work so publicly, even though anonymously, helped me overcome my shyness. The number of followers kept increasing until I received a request to work on a project for Ströck Brot, an Austrian bread manufacturer. That pretty much kicked off my professional career.

Coming from an immigrant family, my parents wished for me to study. And so I did. I studied Graphic Design at a local university, but it didn't shape me as much as it usually shapes others. I was already working on so many projects and actually already running a business. I never had to take a plunge, quit a job, or anything like that. I started showing my work to people so early on that my freelance career evolved organically. In Austria, you can only earn about €10,000 a year before you're required to pay taxes. I realized I was probably making too much money, so one day during break between two lectures, I ran to the offices of the Chamber of Commerce to ask what I needed to do. Five minutes later, on the 12th of April in 2011, I was holding a business license in my hands. Suddenly, I was a business owner.

How is your business set up?
In 2015, I set up a collective with a group of ten friends. We're all solopreneurs. We all work in the creative industries, but we all have a different focus. Because we enjoy working together, we source collaborators from within the group.

While at the beginning I mostly only designed logos and brand identities, I've recently ventured off into interior design. I don't even dare to say what could happen in five or ten years because I never thought interior design would be something I'd ever be asked to do.

Being self-employed, how do you balance your work life?
In our society, it's the norm to grow your business when it's successful. It's the norm to hire more people and take on more responsibility and eventually earn more money. But do you really want all of that? It's often potential clients who put pressure on you and almost demand you hire more people to be able to work on their project. But I really believe that everyone should run the business they feel most comfortable with. A business that suits their individual needs and one they run at their own pace. In my opinion, one doesn't have to run a big business. If my team and I don't have any capacities, then clients must wait. I know for myself that instead of trying to grow my business and measure my success based on my earnings, I define success differently. There's nothing more beautiful than seeing the light and love in the eyes

of my clients when I present them the designs I created for their brand. I love to be the one who gives a face to people's ideas and helps them shape their thoughts. However, there's only so much I can do myself and still savor every moment of the process. I know for myself I can't and don't want to stretch myself too thin.

It sounds better now than what it used to be. I used to get sick a lot. Almost constantly, actually. It took a while for me to realize I couldn't continue working like I was anymore. It wasn't like I woke up one day and had it all figured out. It was a long process of self-reflection and self-discovery to come to a stage of understanding and "knowism." I read a lot of books and talked to a lot of people in a similar situation. Now, I know when you open yourself up and admit that you might need help with something, you'll find the right mentors to guide you through the process.

I changed a few things about my business. First of all, I only do meetings on certain days. I know Monday and Friday will be the days I'll spend talking to a lot of people, but I'll then spend Tuesday to Thursday in my home office. My creative days are a mixture of client work and working on my personal projects. I sleep about ten hours a night, so I start my work days at 11am. I try to finish before 7pm, which works out on most days. As a creative, your head works around the clock, but if you ask me, your hands shouldn't.

Additionally, there are certain things I don't do as a principle. I don't participate in creative pitches, I don't work with intermediary agencies, always with the client directly, and I don't work on projects that don't have good intentions. Also, I definitely don't work with clients that are promising me exposure instead of money. That sort of behavior is clearly unfair and telling me I'm young, and the idea that the exposure would help me run my business is ridiculous. Additionally, besides restructuring my work, I realized I had to take regular breaks to walk away from my computer. I get carried away when working creatively, so it feels natural to stay at my desk, but after feeling the pain in my back, I knew I needed to take action. I bought a laptop I'd only use for leisure that didn't have any design software installed. I also started actively making plans to go to museums, outside, or take short trips to other cities. I had to book trips to really know I'm not going to be home and won't be available for work. Now, I love to take annual sabbaticals.

How would you describe your attitude towards taking time off?
I travel frequently. Sometimes I plan months ahead, and other times I leave spontaneously. When a project takes several weeks, I know that after a big deadline, I'll probably want to take a break. Then I just book a trip somewhere. That's my "me" time!

I've learned how important it is to take breaks and recharge. I used to take on way too much work because I wasn't capable of saying "no." I was too afraid I'd disappoint people. But you have to accept that you can't do it right for others all the time. It's impossible! You simply have to look after yourself. If you don't, no one else will! Now, if I don't have a good gut feeling or realistically can't take on a project because I lack resources, I say "no" immediately. I don't wait. I don't try to squeeze in more hours into the day because while the work results never suffer from me taking on too much work, my health definitely does. At the beginning, it was hard to put myself first because whenever I know I can help, I really want to. However, when you realize you're sick regularly and don't feel your best, it's not because your body is not strong enough. It's because you're asking too much of it. You're a human. Treat yourself accordingly!

If you establish a voice and a style, clients will come to you for that and they'll wait to work with you. Don't get me wrong, I love my work and I love my clients, but I also know how important it is to be good to myself. Just as much as I adore my work, I also love seeing the creations of other people. I love to savor the food of chefs in South Africa, sleep in beautiful hotel rooms in Paris, or enjoy a cocktail carefully crafted in a speakeasy in downtown New York. It's inspiring and it helps me create better work while also taking time off.

How did you start implementing travel into your work life after you went freelance?

When I accept a project, I know how long it will take, so I might simultaneously book a city trip to make sure I relax my thoughts for a little. I also book trips in between bigger projects. When I know a project is coming to an end, I go somewhere right after and before I start working on the next one to start with a clear head.

You have to have the courage and really be the one who's in charge of your agenda. You're your own boss; it's your job to make sure you take time to relax!

How do you communicate to your clients you're not going to be available?

When I take on a new project, I estimate a deadline. Even if I work in a team for a project, I'm the one who communicates with the client. I know that as long as we deliver on time, no one cares if we take a break in between or not. In 2015, I left on an inspirational break for several months and the out of office message read:

Dear sender,
We're currently on an inspirational break and will be back in the office on XYZ. All emails and calls will be answered after our return. In urgent cases, get a margarita!
Enjoy your summer,
#teamkarasinski
www.atelierkarasinski.com
www.instagram.com/laurakarasinski

And while I was originally worried about being so casual, people responded very positively. The best clients get us, and even my tax consultant called up to say how joyful she thought the message was!

How does it work out financially for you?

While money is important, of course, I try to focus as much time as I can on being creative and as little time as possible on the administrative side of my business. I have a modular system for how I charge for different services. The quotes with their prices are prefabricated. After the first appointment, I send out a quote and the client can choose the services they want. Given I know I'm not a numbers person, when I first started my business, I immediately hired a tax consultant. When hiring a tax advisor, you should make sure they're more than just a service provider; you want an ally who gets you and looks out for you. I know how much money I need and I know I need to earn a little more than twice that amount to be able to cover taxes and health insurance. Usually, whatever I put aside is what I end up paying to the government anyway. Whenever I need money, I take out money. Whenever I get a bill, I pay it. I don't want to increase my workload. I'm satisfied with how much I have and I know how much is enough.

How do you budget for your travels?

I don't budget. I have a safety cushion and as long as I'm above that, I know I can follow my wanderlust.

What's something you'd recommend to others who want to start traveling, even if they have too much work on their plate?

Ask for help! There are plenty of other people who could step in for you. You should be fair to yourself and acknowledge that it's better to say "no" instead of delivering work that's below your means or robs you of your sleep! Get to know yourself, embrace your strengths, charge what you deserve, and get help for the things that take up too much of your time without the appropriate return in value. Just simply acknowledge how much you're capable of and delegate everything else to others. The two most important things in life are that you don't turn into an asshole and that you stay healthy. Put your health first and do so at all times.

Laura Karasinski on
Web: atelierkarasinski.com
Instagram: @laurakarasinski

YASMINE
ÅKERMARK

BE FULLY PRESENT

What's been your educational and professional path?
When I finished high school, everyone said I should either study law, politics, or economics. I decided to do the latter. It's not necessarily that I wanted to study economics. It was more of a decision based on what others said I should do. Even though I'm interested in macroeconomics and the politics impacting economics, to be completely honest, if I was to make the decision on what to study today, I'd probably enroll in something more creative.

My mother always wished for me to have a stable life; a proper job, a proper house. It's funny because she's the one who put me on the back of an elephant when I was six months old and made me move to different countries throughout my entire childhood. What did she expect would happen? I feel she set the standards for me at a very early stage in life. Thanks to her, I can easily adapt to change.

As far as I can remember, I've always been traveling and living in different countries. I've consciously applied to internships and jobs in other countries. I think it's the easiest way to get around. I've done internships in France and Malaysia, and I've also worked in the UK while still in school. Once I graduated, I applied for a job at the World Trade Organization in Switzerland and later on, I moved to work at the World Trade Center in France. My career was going well. On paper anyway! However, in reality, I worked in a highly bureaucratic environment. Things were moving very slowly. Quite frankly, it wasn't the most inspiring place. For fun and to keep myself inspired, I set up a side business; an online store for sustainable clothing. Working on my side project enabled me to make full use of my skills, from the graphics and the website, to the photography. I created a playground that enabled me to hone my skills.

Even though I studied economics, I wouldn't say I'm necessarily good at it. My thing really is the creative side of running a business. When I decided to no longer climb the corporate ladder and instead switch careers to do something that was more up my alley, I didn't need to start from scratch because I already had my online store. I then additionally set up a creative agency to help other small businesses with their branding.

How is your business set up?

I split my time between building my own business, Tibba, which is a bartering network to help people trade skills instead of money, and I also work in the creative agency that I cofounded, which helps small businesses with their online presence. Tibba is a shared venture with my friend, Erica Werneman, that we came up with while traveling.

I've always bartered because I never had too much money to do all the cool things I wanted to do. I realized a platform like Tibba would make it less awkward to ask people to trade instead of buying what they offered. It's not a platform to help cover the basic needs in life; instead, it's a way for people who want to trade their skills for all sorts of adventures.

While Tibba requires my attention full-time, I also do creative work on the side to be able to keep going because we haven't found a way to monetize Tibba yet. The creative agency is a business I run with another friend. For Burp Creative, we found a niche by mainly working with Scandinavian clients that wanted to break through or were already present in the British market. A lot of our clients are retainer clients and we like to keep working with everyone we accept as a long-term client. While my friend focuses on the customer-facing part of the business, I do all the creative work. Additionally, I have a couple of clients that I work with independently. The nature of the businesses I've started enables me to be location independent.

How would you describe your attitude towards travel?
I love traveling by myself. Sure, it can get lonely at times, which might then be overwhelming, but I know it's the sort of lifestyle I really want for myself. When you're on your own, you must be much more sociable to get to know new people. Being by yourself also allows you to completely immerse in the culture you're in. You don't have anyone to hold on to who would give you the sort of comfort of the familiar. It's just you and you must be fully present.

There are pros and cons to being a solo female traveler. Social media reminds you a lot of how your life should be, especially when you're hitting your thirties. You're constantly presented with all the things you're supposed to be and all the things you're supposed to have at that age. However, for me, I know that if I had a husband, a house, and a secure job, I'd probably feel restless.

I love the overwhelming feeling you get when you come to a new city. I love chaos. I love the air. It's all like an explosion of colors and feelings. Being on the road just makes me feel alive! Once, I was stuck on an island somewhere near the coast of Malaysia without having a cent on me. Of course, they didn't take cards! What was I thinking? So for two days straight, I needed to barter my way through. Another time, I was on a plane from Saudi Arabia to Ethiopia and I was wrapped in a persian carpet because I was so cold. It's those moments that make me crave more adventures! Simultaneously, this sort of chaos and discovery makes me come back to London every so often.

Given I'm bootstrapping a company, I travel on a budget, which doesn't mean I plan and book everything in advance. I mostly go to places spontaneously and once I arrive, I see where life takes me. For the past couple of years, I've had a base in London that I go back to for about five to six months each year. For the rest of the year, I'm mostly living somewhere else. It's rare for me to just go somewhere for a month. I really like hanging out in places for much longer. Having a room in London enables me to have somewhere to come back to and store the things that I can't take with me on the road. I share the house with a friend, and that enables me to sublet my room whenever I leave. Most of the time, I'm gone for a couple of months. It's easy to find someone to sublet when you know you won't return for three or four months. If I leave for just a couple of weeks, I put my room up on Airbnb. When I go somewhere, I look for cheap flight tickets and then book an Airbnb in an area that I think will be cool. If the return flights are much cheaper than just a one-way ticket or if a return flight is required to be able to enter a country, I'll book a return flight immediately. Otherwise, I'll do it on the fly and just see how much I like a place and if I want to stay longer. Once I arrive at a new location, I start connecting with locals. I'll look for groups on meetup.com to learn more about the creative scene and what sort of events and festivals are happening while I'm going to live there. The digital nomad scene has grown in the past couple of years and there are some very useful Slack chats I'm a part of. Look for the Nomad List, various Facebook groups, such as Digital Nomads Around The World, if you're curious!

I often skim through Facebook groups before I go somewhere new. Sometimes, I search for local coworking spaces. They're great if you want to become familiar with the local tech communities. Most of them also have an events section on their website.

When it comes to housing, even though I might want to explore the entire country and probably also some of the neighboring countries, I'll still make sure to have a base for the entire stay. I like having a place I can go back to, so I'll book a place and then go on shorter trips. I really love having the ability to take my work anywhere.

How did you start implementing travel into your work life after you went freelance?

Once I quit my job at the World Trade Center, I tried to find another "normal" job. It didn't work out very well! I had three normal jobs within a month: I got fired from the first one, I quit the second one, and with the third one, the company went bankrupt. So, I'd say it simply wasn't meant to be. I tried to do what I was supposed to do, what my mom wanted me to do. What society tells you to do. But thinking I should get a proper job and then having those proper jobs was really killing me. I had to quiet what society thinks one is supposed to do and trust what my instincts were telling me. It was truly a path I dared to take.

Somehow, I've always known I'm not someone who'd be content with a normal 9-to-5 kind of job. Traveling is what makes me happiest, so I decided to go freelance and bring my work with me wherever I went. There are all sorts of quotes on the internet telling you that you only have one life and you could die tomorrow. And you know what? It's true!

I really hate missing out on opportunities. I know some people who have stable jobs and they just want to go on vacation for two weeks every year, but that just doesn't apply to how I want to live my life. I used to earn a decent salary and I'd look forward to every single weekend and every single bank holiday, but to me, I really prefer to have less money and do what I want to do at all times.

It took a long time for me to realize I could do that; that I could travel and still make enough money to support myself. The term "digital nomad" wasn't a thing until very recently. I always tried to get a real job, but then I panicked because it really wasn't my thing. Now, I know I'd much rather deal with the scariness of being location independent and running my own business than working at a company that asks me to show up at the office every morning.

I believe that once you focus your energy on the lifestyle you want to create for yourself, you can make it a reality. I first started taking on small projects and then I moved into a cheaper apartment. I really explored the small bits and pieces that helped me save money and enabled me to create an independent lifestyle. I love being able to follow my heart and jump at opportunities as they come my way.

How do you communicate to your clients you're not going to be available?

Generally, I prefer to handle communication with clients over email. I prefer to have a record of what's been said. If, however, calls are necessary, I have my cofounder handle it, so I mostly only Skype with people when we first meet to get to know them better.

I admit, sometimes, written communication leads to confusion. If my business partner meets a client, there might be some details that get lost in the funnel, but it's still better for me to organize my workload like that because I don't necessarily work on the same schedule as others. I like to work in the evenings or during the weekends. I might then take a day off when others are working.

A big part of my work is attending events. Especially when I go to new places, I try to get to know as many people as possible. For that, I try to find different types of events in each city. I go to some events with the aim of meeting potential investors for Tibba, and I go to other events to find clients for my agency business. Most of our agency clients came either through referrals or because we met them at an event. We really only want to work with like-minded people. Just the idea of trying to find people through personalized, yet cold emails feels scary to me. I'm not a fan of spammy emails. For me, finding new clients has really mostly worked through personal recommendations. With such clients, I already know we'll be okay because as long as I deliver as promised, no one will care where in the world I am.

Being self-employed, how do you balance your work life?

That's something I struggle with a lot. To me, it really feels like I'm always traveling and I'm always working. Sometimes, I turn off my phone. That's on the good days. I'm also not available for two or three hours before going to bed. In the mornings, I leave my phone off for another two hours; however, I'm always very tempted to check it. What I realized works best is going to places where I don't have reception.

One thing I did in the past was I went on a silent meditation retreat in the desert. It was really great, but also extraordinarily challenging. During the first two days, I really thought I was going to die. Meditating for ten hours a day without any sort of distraction is one of the hardest things I've done in my life. Being quiet wasn't actually that hard; you get used to it. But being in the same position for ten hours a day was closer to hitting my personal boundaries than anything else I've experienced.

How does it work out financially for you?

One of the reasons I keep leaving London is that the city is incredibly pricey. There's always a moment when I'm too poor to stay. London, from my experience, requires you to hustle a lot, so every time I realize I'm running out of cash and might need to dip into my savings, I know it's time to go elsewhere.

When I'm in other places, I usually manage to save a lot of money. Over time, I've worked out how much on average I spend each day. I have full control over my finances. I know my income and I know my spendings. For years, I've had a morning ritual of writing down how much I spent the day before. There are apps, such as *MoneyBook*, that make it easy to keep control over your finances. However, I personally prefer to use pen and paper. Being so aware of my finances gives me some sort of security because I know how much I can afford or when it's time for me to grab the cheaper groceries at the supermarket.

I don't measure success based on earnings. To me, what matters is how many people are on board with what we're trying to create with Tibba. The money I make from freelancing is just to survive; what matters are the people who want to make a change towards a more focused society. I've always bartered a lot. For example, I stayed at a place for free because I taught French to the children of the family I was staying with. At first, I was just asking people if they needed help with something that I was able to give to them; French lessons, web design, you name it! I guess that's also why I founded Tibba. Asking around is pretty much something only extroverts would consider doable! So, in my opinion, Tibba makes bartering much easier because people can see other personality types barter too!

How do you budget for your travels?
When I was still running an ecommerce business, I was making around €6,000 a month after taxes. Back then, I knew that wasn't going to go on forever, so I saved up the majority of my income. I knew I could've gotten a much nicer apartment and eaten out at much fancier restaurants, but I had a feeling saving the money I was making was a more sensible thing to do. I simply knew that money could help me achieve other things, so I wanted to live on as little as possible.

In the past two years, even though I was still earning money from my freelance assignments, I've also been able to supplement my income through my previous earnings from the time I worked in ecommerce. For me, it's easy to keep a budget and actually live by it because I'm so very aware of my financial situation. I know how much I want to spend each week. When I travel to Asia, I know a place to stay will cost me £10 a night, and I'll probably need another £10 for food each day. I know I have £150 pounds each week that I shouldn't exceed. If I happen to spend £100 in one night, I know I only have £50 left for the rest of the week. And I take that count seriously! I've been earning more and more money over time and because I work with retainer clients; I know how much to expect each month. I used to undercharge people when I first started, but now I know the value of my work. Having been a freelancer for a couple of years, I ask for more money and I'm also able to save the extra income, either for a rainy day or for me to be able to focus on building and expanding Tibba.

What's something you'd recommend to others who want to travel the way you do?

I've learned that what holds many of us back is fear. There are so many people who have so much potential. They're so much smarter than I am; they could do everything I do and probably do a much better job at it, but their fear holds them back.

A lot of times, you can get whatever you want if you just ask for it. If you really want to travel and also work, you need to adapt your job search for that sort of criteria. Or you can ask your boss if you could work from somewhere else for a month. Just start small. The worst that can happen is they'll say "no."

Yasmine Åkermark on
Web: tibba.co
Instagram: @travelyas

NATALIE HOWARD

THINK OF
YOUR BIGGER
GOAL!

What's been your educational and professional path?

When I was deciding what I wanted to study, there was just one school I was interested in. I only applied to this one school and got in. I studied Visual Communications at a fashion school in LA because I wanted to become a stylist for TV shows and movies. However, when you decide on a career you believe you want to have, you hardly ever decide on the sort of lifestyle you want. Many of us decide on a job because of the status it brings them. I quickly realized I didn't want to have a career that was extremely unstable and required me to work up to 18 hours a day. It was unfortunate because this particular school got me into a lot of debt.

When I discovered my love for travel, I knew I needed to find a career that was flexible and would eventually allow me to become location independent. I love traveling by myself and doing whatever I want, taking part in activities I enjoy, or leaving early if I don't feel a place is right for me.

I've always had entrepreneurial ambitions, but none of my business ideas ever felt 100% right because none of them would allow me to work from anywhere. Then, a friend recommended to read *The Four-Hour Work Week* by Tim Ferris, and after I read it, I knew this was the sort of business I needed to build for myself; a business I could take with me anywhere.

As an alternative to working as a stylist, I taught myself graphic design before going back to school after about a year of working full-time to study Interactive Media Design.

Once I finished school, I quit my job to take a sabbatical. I'd been saving for a trip to New Zealand for a couple of months and it seemed like a great opportunity to hit the road. My plan was to stay until I ran out of money. I ended up staying in New Zealand for one month, and then jetted over to Bali for another month.

When I came back, it was time for me to face reality; in other words, my student loans. I needed to get serious.

How is your business set up?

Currently, I work full-time at a corporate company. I'm a contractor because it leaves me more flexibility and I can ask for more money compared to what I'd earn as a regular employee. After I get home from my day job, I work on building my own business.

Next to my freelance design projects, I work as a plus size model, and because I have a respectable following online, I've been getting more and more Instagram sponsorships and support via Patreon, which is a platform for creators to get paid while creating. Fans pay a few dollars per month or per post creators' release. I'm really focused on monetizing my online presence. Even though I would really love to be a digital nomad, I first need to tackle my six figure student loan. I'm definitely in hustle mode right now! My plan is to pay off my loans within the next five years.

I'm not someone who likes to sacrifice a certain lifestyle. I'd much rather make sure I earn more instead of holding myself back. If I want to have a drink with friends, I'll simply have a drink with friends. That's the sort of freedom I don't want to give up. However, my loan is my priority! I'm making really good money with my day job, and then I focus on my side businesses to pay the loan off much faster. As an entrepreneur, there's no cap to your earnings. Anything is possible if you figure out the right system. I once heard that "job" stands for "just over broke," which made a lot of sense to me. Companies try to pay you as little as possible for your time. I've realized that if you work on a per project basis, you're often much faster and end up earning more. Another deal breaker for me is that in a regular job, you only get two weeks of vacation, which is definitely not enough in my opinion. A job is usually sold to you under the promise that it's safer. I don't actually think so. I really think it's an illusion because if the economy changes, your job might change with it. As a contractor, if you do a good job, they'll want to keep you on and if you get a better offer, you don't have any hard feelings about leaving. It's also not a big deal to pay for your own health insurance.

Being a contractor has allowed me to focus on my modeling career. I feel very passionate about improving women's body images. People might say it's trivial, but it truly is foundational to many women. If they don't love and feel good about themselves, it's harder for them to build that confidence to get ahead in life.

In 2014, I became absorbed in the plus size community and signed up with a plus size model agency. To promote my career, I started using Facebook where I'd share snapshots from my photo shoots. The feedback was phenomenal! I'd get emails telling me I was brave for showing myself in underwear, and the women who were writing me would say they wouldn't even go to a pool because they hated how they looked in bikinis too much. I knew how important the work I was doing actually was.

I really want to support women and help them feel better about themselves and their bodies. I want people to see that there's not just one standard of beauty, but that it's really diverse.

When Facebook's growth slowed down, I moved over to Instagram, and once the interaction on Instagram became unmanageable for me, I began focusing on Patreon, where I have a more selected group of fans who pay me for my engagement.

I really want to normalize different body shapes in our society. I'd love to become an icon for body acceptance and body positivity. It's a big part of why I'm doing what I'm doing. I have a mentor and a manager who help me figure out how I can scale my business. We try to figure out different strategies and it's a lot of fun! We've been looking at what sort of fans I have to understand the demographics; what jobs they have, where they come from. On my laptop, I keep spreadsheets where I track content ideas because I ask my fans for a lot of input. I also keep an Amazon wishlist where people can buy what looks I have on, and I'll then take pictures wearing the dresses they buy.

The way I see social media work is that you should take care of what you have from day one. Then, your following will grow. I've always been very personal in the way I've responded to people's questions and comments. I make an effort to show I care, and I look at other people's posts too. I want them to know I pay attention to them. Over time, my following has become too big to give everyone a reasonable amount of attention, which is why Patreon has been so great. If people really want to interact with me and they become part of my community on Patreon, I need to make it my priority. The question you should always ask yourself is what do you have that people might find useful and interesting? If not for money, you can also always barter your skills. When I was younger, I wanted to move out, so I posted an ad on Craigslist that I wanted to trade free graphic designs for free rent. It might sound weird, but it actually worked out really well. I lived in a house of an entrepreneur who was fixing up houses and selling them, and I did the graphic design work for him while living in a really good area of town for a year.

How would you describe your attitude towards travel?
I only got out of school at the beginning of January 2016. Because I've been working and going to school full-time, once I started exploring the world, I became obsessed. I remember I had friends who were traveling a lot and I kept wondering how they were able to afford all their trips. Instead of just checking out their Instagram stream, I checked out their website, and there I found a link to a travel hacking course they were trying to sell to teach others how to use credit cards to collect points to pay for flights. I googled "travel hacking" and that really opened the door to me. I didn't end up buying their course because it was a bit too pricey for me, and I

realized I could invest a little bit more time and find free resources instead. I always thought I couldn't explore the world until I was in my 30s or 40s because of my student loans, but once I learned how cheap travel could be, it really felt like there were no excuses!

A good trick for when you want to figure something out is to look at the sort of terms someone uses and then refine your Google queries. After learning about travel hacking, I started applying for credit cards. This is mostly an American thing because outside the US, there are not that many companies that have great deals for travelers. If you've ever wondered how some people are able to afford extensive travel, this might be an explanation: there are a lot of travel credit cards, like for Southwest Airlines or the more known banks, such as Chase, who offer travel credit cards. There really are a ton of different cards, so you need to look for the ones that will suit your needs and sign up.

In order for you to get the bonuses these companies promise, you often need to fulfil certain requirements. For example, you might have to spend $1,000 within 90 days in order to get the promised points, which could be as much as 50,000 miles. My rule has always been that I'd only sign up for credit cards I could actually afford. Then, I'd take these cards to pay for the things I'd buy anyway, such as gas, groceries, and rent. In order for me to keep track of my cards, I started a spreadsheet where I noted all the credit accounts I opened, the requirements, when to cancel them, and my progress. I got up to 250,000 miles, which has paid for most of my international flights and saved me several thousand dollars. It's definitely been a valuable hobby.

I started collecting miles about three or four months before I was able to book my first flight overseas. The way it worked was that I had a card where for anything travel-related you bought with that card, the company gave you $450 towards your statement. I found a $400 round trip flight to Milan and that's how I got my first trip to Europe for free. I also used these miles to go on trips across the US to visit friends. Before, hopping on a plane for the weekend to see my friends in LA seemed like luxury, but with free miles, it suddenly became very doable. When I travel, I like staying at Airbnbs because I prefer to have a private room. It's also turned out to be an incredibly reliable solution to stay in different places. I love meeting locals, so next to Airbnb, I also use Couchsurfing to meet people in different cities. When I come to a new place, I look for Couchsurfers in the area and ask them out for a coffee. I've had some incredible experiences where they took me out for drinks, played tour guide for me, accompanied me to a museum, or even invited me to their friend's private party.

How did you start implementing travel into your work life after you went freelance?
Currently, I'm not traveling as much as I'd love to. As I said, my loan is my first priority. Before I decided to be disciplined and focused, I'd go somewhere every month or every other month.

I love to be spontaneous when I travel. A lot of people get caught up in planning and they get paralyzed. I really think that you just have to stop planning and start doing. I do keep a list of interesting places on Pinterest; there are a lot of valuable travel guides. I also keep a spreadsheet with countries I want to visit, the sights I want to see there, and the names of friends and friends of friends that I can stay with in various destinations. It's a loose outline because I don't like to have too much of an itinerary when I go somewhere. I want to be surprised. I really like being delighted by exploring.

I usually travel between contracts. At the moment, when I travel for the sake of travel, I only do some small things for my freelance clients I've had for years while on the road. My next step is definitely to transition into a digital nomad lifestyle and work while traveling.

How do you communicate to your clients you're only there for a limited period of time?
Every time I interview with a corporate company and they ask me

what I'm looking for in a position, I'm very upfront about work-life balance and flexibility being really important to me. For example, I ask them if there's a chance for me to work out of a coffee shop some days. Once they know you're doing your job, you can ask for more. I prefer to start small and take it from there. I also only take on contract work because then I can take as much time off as I need.

Being so focused on paying back your loan, how do you keep your wanderlust in check?
I ask myself two questions. What do I need to be happy? What can I do in Columbus that I enjoy doing? Travel is about having a variety of experiences and meeting new people, so I started a group on meetup.com that is targeted at full-time freelancers and digital nomads. I've found that taking a leadership role can be very rewarding. I surround myself with people that inspire me. It's very satisfying, even though it gives me a different kind of satisfaction.

Reminding myself of the good times I had on the road and knowing I want more of that helps me stay disciplined. I know I'm doing this for the long-term gain. I'm finding so much satisfaction with my side business I'm creating and love coming home in the evening to a quiet house that allows me to recharge and work on projects I'm looking forward to. Even though I'm tired from my day job, I'm excited to work on my own projects. I can see the results of my work immediately and I can also see that if I don't do anything for my side business, not much happens. Monetizing social media might look very serendipitous from the outside, but there's often very strict planning behind it. Of course, it's not like I work all the time; I go out for drinks with friends, or watch a movie too!

Many others would probably say it's impossible to do anything outside of their regular nine-to-five, but I've come to realize that doing yoga helps a lot with managing your energy. I know if I skip yoga, I feel tired and unmotivated, so I've been doing yoga with the help of twenty minutes videos I'd find on Youtube. I can recommend PsycheTruth's channel.

How do you budget for your travels?

I wouldn't say I do, which is I guess why I've gotten into trouble. If you have to look at your expenses while you travel, that kind of kills the fun for me. For my trip to New Zealand, I budgeted $5,000 for two months and I did pretty well with that. Once I only had $1,500 left in my bank account, I knew it was time for me to go home because that was the money I needed to live off of until I found another job. I really think that when you want to travel, you need at least two or three thousand left in your bank account as a safety cushion to be able to cover your flights back home and some extra money until you're set up to earn more money again.

One of my favorite tools to manage my finances is Mint, which again, is an American invention. I check my balances every single day because it helps me stay on a budget. It's a weird trick, but if you're really aware of your finances, you'll be much more disciplined and responsible about how you spend your money.

If you want to get into travel hacking, you need to be meticulous and document everything to make sure you don't end up spending more money than you can afford. Over time, I've had 15 to 20 credit cards to collect miles, but you really need to make sure you read all the small print before you get into this. To keep my travel budget in check, I use Google Sheets. Then, I use Skyscanner to find cheap flight deals. The way I use Skyscanner is I look for flights that go out of the US and where the destination is pretty much anywhere in the world. The more flexible you are, the better because you can find deals for the entire year. If I find an incredibly cheap deal to Iceland, I'll just book it and go to Iceland.

What's something you'd recommend to others who want to travel the way you do?

So many people tell you to quit your job and travel the world, but it's more complicated than that. Do your research, look up good deals, be flexible, and start small. You don't have to travel the entire world all at once!

Natalie Howard on
Web: nhoward.com
Instagram: @nataliereneeplus

I mean, we couldn't have avoided this for any longer.
Let's crunch some numbers!

- *How much do you need to earn? In a month? In a year?*

- *How much do you want to earn per month, per year?*

- *How much money is enough money?*

- *What are you saving up for?*

- *What are some considerable possibilities for you to build scalable income streams?*

- *Which of your expenses can you eliminate or reduce?*

- *What's your plan for this year to increase your financial literacy?*

ABOUT
TRAVEL

When we travel, when we're on the road in between places or when we're on vacation, we allow ourselves to be in the moment. It's one of the things I love most about traveling. We soak up everything around us, and we get excited about the tiniest details we'd easily overlook if they were in the streets where we live. What travel does to us is special!

When I decided to write about travel, my aim was to shed some light on the perspective of life as a journey. Given that freelancing enables you to make every day different, I figured combining the topics of work and travel would make for an interesting read. I admit, the majority of this book has been about what you need to think about, what there is to be considered, and what you should plan for. Partly, while rereading my words, I thought how stressful I made freelancing sound at times.

However, travel planning is stressful. When you travel, you usually make some sort of a plan beforehand. In one way or another, you either make a budget or at least give yourself a limit for how much is okay for you to spend. You think about what you'll do while you're there. You might even read a travel guide to get an idea of what it's like at your desired destination. See the parallels?

Now, and for the final part of this book, I actually do want to talk about travel. I want to make you think about the places you'd love to visit and the places you'd like to live in for some time. I want to use this final chapter to talk about solo (female) travel about moving abroad, about traveling while working. I want to talk about taking time off. Generally, I want to clarify the difference between what it means to travel and what it means to take a vacation. They are most certainly not the same. I also want to take a closer look at what it is that makes travel so special and explain how you could implement those elements into your everyday life.

In recent years, it's become more accessible to bring our work on the road. We no longer have to sit in an office to call what we do work. For many, all we need to deliver good results is a laptop and wifi. It's never been easier to see the world without needing rich parents. Sure, you need to have courage and some organizational skills. Travel demands you to be agile, reactive, and resourceful.

Taking your work on the road most certainly requires for you to be self-confident and have trust in yourself. You need to be able to trust that with whatever happens, you'll be able to figure things out. You know that if your plan A fails, that you'll still be able to come up with a plan B, C, or even D.

I hope the following pages give you some additional ideas and inspire you to go somewhere new, or maybe revisit somewhere you've been before. You most certainly can!

Ready to take off?

1 TAKE TIME OFF

———

The best thing about being self-employed is that you can take as much time off as you want! Theoretically, anyway, because it's known that freelancers have a hard time claiming their freedom. Most of us have an always-on mindset, and even when we go on vacation, we still tempt to sneak in some work hours and reply to a couple of emails. It's our business, so we feel like we must, but do we really? Is it really necessary to reply to all of our emails immediately? Is it necessary to be always on? I'd say it's not! And no, you don't! Emails can wait!

There are many advantages to being self-employed. You don't have to head out on the most expensive flight days of the week, but can leave on a Tuesday or Wednesday, which are typically the cheapest days to fly. Once you get back from a vacation, you don't need to go back to your regular work hours right away. You can sleep when the jet lag hits you, and then do your work when it suits your body. You don't even have to get back to work after two weeks. You can go away for much longer if your budget allows for it. However, you might still disagree or need more convincing, so here are seven simple tips to how you can prepare for a stress-free vacation as freelancer:

Observe when it's high and low demand season for your work
If you aren't a freelancer newbie, then you've definitely noticed that there are times when you get more requests and other times when no one seems to need your services. Observe when that is, make notes in your calendar, and plan to go on vacation when you know no one will call you!

Plan your vacation way in advance
Decide when you'll go on vacation way ahead of time and book your flights to make sure you'll really take off. Just like anyone, you need time to recharge and reflect on what you're doing with your life too.

Be flexible about your destination
Skyscanner has a tool that enables you to determine what month you want to leave, and then look for destinations accordingly. You don't have to go to the most expensive spot just because it's the one destination everyone seems to go to that's all over Instagram. Be flexible and find the best deal that suits your needs!

Tell your clients in advance when you won't be available
Reach out to your clients proactively and tell them you won't be available for two weeks, or even longer, about a month before your departure. Ask them whether they have work they'll need you to take care of before you leave.

Update your email signature
About two weeks prior to your departure, include a note in your email signature to remind people when you won't be reachable via email. Communication is key!

Turn on your OoO notice two days before your planned departure
Give yourself space to finish things up. By turning on your OoO reminder two days before your departure, you won't feel pressured to respond to emails that trickle in at the very last minute when you really need to be packing!

Turn off email on your phone
If there's one thing I've learned while working in advertising, it's that no one's going to die if you don't respond within 24 hours! You're a creative, not a doctor. You don't have to be available 24/7! You've

communicated to everyone you'll be on vacation. Allow yourself to be fully present!

See? It's not that hard! If you've saved up to allow yourself to take time off, I'm pretty sure you'll be able to pick up work wherever you left it. As Becky said, there will always be work for you to do, so don't you worry and off you go!

2 GO NOMAD

───

If you crave leaving the comfort of your home to go on adventures more often than just for a couple of weeks a year, why don't you head out and explore the world, but take your work with you? Once you have clients you work for regularly who already know you, it doesn't usually matter whether you're in the same city or not. Nowadays, a lot of jobs have the advantage that you can work from anywhere. If you have a niche, and the better you've positioned yourself in your branch, the easier it will be to find clients despite your location.

One of the most wonderful things about freelancing is that you're in charge, and if you allow yourself to claim the freedom that comes with being self-employed, you can do almost anything you set out to do.

From what I've observed, there seem to be two types of approaches to becoming a digital nomad. Some people save up to go to Asia or where it's cheaper to live than where they're from. They develop a bootstrap business model aimed at the western world that, even if it's small with just a few clients or paying customers, pay them enough to get by. Others build a business and establish healthy working relationships with their clients back home, or have a product that already sells. Then, they go location independent because they have an appetite for exploration and their work allows them to fully embrace their travel bug.

Given that long-term travel is something many do by themselves or, if possible, with their partners, some places have become popular for location independent workers. Places where it's easy to find temporary homes. Places with good working infrastructure. Places where meeting other like-minded people requires almost no effort. Cities like Chiang Mai, Ubud, and Saigon might be the most popular ones in Asia.

People also love to hang out in Berlin, Barcelona, or Sofia. These cities, despite being in Europe, are relatively affordable. Oaxaca in Mexico, Medellín in Colombia, and Puerto Viejo in Costa Rica are the most popular hot spots in the Americas. You can find many groups for digital nomads on Facebook or join The Nomad List on Slack if you'd like to research this topic in more depth.

If you feel like you're drawn to this sort of lifestyle, it's certainly not necessary to leave for good on day one. You don't have to sell everything and become a full-time nomad right away. You can try things out and see if you like being on the road for more than just a couple of weeks. Only if you try this sort of lifestyle out yourself will you be able to see whether you enjoy living away from home in the first place.

While it's wonderful to see the world and experience different cultures, you're relinquishing the chance to be with your friends and family and participate in their lives. But then, no one said that if you go nomadic, you must be nomadic forever. Life is about making it a worthwhile journey! As the title of this book implies, life is about embracing all the road trips and work trips equally.

When Stephanie (whose story you'll soon read) left the US, she didn't intend to become a digital nomad. She went on a vacation and decided she wanted to stay on the road longer. The same goes for Kaitlyn. She didn't intend to live on Airbnbs for years when she went on her first cross-Atlantic trip to Paris. She just liked how it was to work while traveling, so she and her partner built their careers around their desired lifestyle.

You might've noticed that once you set your mind to something, opportunities seem to pop up everywhere. Once you have an idea you think is cool, chances will often line up for you. (Most likely because you also look for them!) Then, all you need to do is claim these chances!

When I asked everyone what their final advice to you was, they all said you have to overcome your fears and just go. Which is so true! It's most certainly fear that's stopping us from pursuing certain things in life.

An approach I find interesting to how to best conquer your fears is something I read in Tim Ferriss book, *The Tools of Titans*. Tim suggested to deconstruct your fears by implementing them in your everyday life. Many, for example, fear losing social status and their wealth. It was something Tim feared as well, so he started to sleep in a sleeping bag on the floor of his apartment. He only wore white shirts and one pair of jeans. He used Couchsurfing to stay with people for free, and he ate instant oatmeal and rice with beans to cut his costs, all to make himself feel what he dreaded most: being poor. Now, of course, this isn't comparable to what actual poverty is. What Tim tried was living on a super tight budget while remaining a part of his social infrastructure. But, was it really that bad? No, it wasn't! He came to the conclusion that if his biggest fears weren't that bad, he could most certainly push the boundaries of his own comfort much harder. As he said, and what most resonated with me, was his insight that "there's more freedom to be gained from practicing poverty than chasing wealth."

Your fear might not be poverty. Your fear might be something else. It's only you who can look into deconstructing your fears in order to overcome them in your own way, on your own terms.

When you travel by yourself, you have the chance to test your boundaries. Fearing to be lonely or having some other fear shouldn't be what stops you. The only good reason why you shouldn't try this, even for a little, would be because you're not interested.

What I believe is important, and how I'd like to close this chapter off, is by telling you that living wherever you live is a choice, not a given, and it's in your hands to change that. You can move on. Anytime. Yes, you can do that. And yes, you can head out if that's what your heart's craving. Whatever you believe is holding you back is an illusion you've constructed yourself. Break it apart!

3 HEAD OUT BY YOURSELF

———

Have you ever traveled by yourself? Have you ever gone to a restaurant and asked for a table for one? Have you ever gone to the cinema alone? Chances are, you haven't, but why not?

There seems to be a stigma about people who spend time by themselves. However, being with yourself in solitude is when you get to know the real you. It's when you learn to trust yourself and test what you're capable of. When you do things by yourself, or even travel alone, you allow your different personality traits to come to the surface. When you're on your own, you don't fear judgement from people whose opinions you value and don't want to disappoint.

It's much easier to free yourself from the social stigma if you allow yourself to step out of your everyday and your community's social norms to observe what it's like and what's considered normal somewhere else. When you're young, and especially as a female, you were told everything that's supposedly dangerous. But people, regardless of their skin color, most likely want the same thing: to share a good life with the people around them.

Sure, there are moments and social standards that are opposite from yours. There are some situations that might be unpleasant or potentially even dangerous, but I believe that if you use your common sense, it's likely nothing bad will happen to you.

Breaking out of your safe zone and pushing through the idea that you'll hit the road by yourself to go to places as far as Egypt or Thailand might be the part that will require the most courage. From then on, it will be easy! By now, you've read enough stories in this book that prove just that. One reason why you might've never liked going places by yourself is because you've feared to remain alone. There are places where it might be harder to get to know people. Nevertheless, this sort of fear is unfounded. From my experience, once you're by yourself, you're more approachable. If you're somewhere new, you lose that determined look on your face that signals to others you know where you're going and would prefer being left alone. If you're novel somewhere, and this applies to smaller towns probably even more than it does to big towns, you're unknown and thus, exciting.

I once traveled to Thirsk, which is in the middle of the British countryside. I went there all by myself to visit the James Herriot museum (yes, I truly am obsessed). I found a young family on Couchsurfing and they opened their home to me. More than that, they actually took me around to show me their town they were most certainly proud of. They introduced me to everyone with, "This is Monika. She's our Couchsurfer. Yes, she's staying with us for a couple of days." They loved that! I did too. Everyone in that town of not even 5,000 residents could clearly see I didn't belong. They all loved chatting with me and were extraordinarily friendly. Everyone recommended to me where I should go and what I should see. Being alone was easy because I wasn't alone at all!

There's a difference between people who go somewhere (or even board a plane) that want to be left alone and people who seek conversations. Whenever you enter a place, look around for people you think might enjoy chatting to you. Go to places where they don't have tiny tables for two, but bigger tables to share. Then, turn around and make a note about someone's necklace, their bag, or ask them what they're working on and why they're there. It really doesn't matter what you say!

It often feels like we've lost the guts to just walk across the room to talk to people. All too often, we rely on technology to help us introduce ourselves, even though some of the most memorable moments happen when someone talks to you unexpectedly.
It's in your hands to be that person!

It's up to you to be the person that's remembered. At first, you might be intimidated to chat with people in your own age group, so aim for older ladies or gentlemen. They will most certainly enjoy being regarded by someone your age; they'll be grateful you paid attention. Over time, it will be easier to chat to just about anyone. In my opinion, it's all a matter of practice. It's actually almost humorous (and somehow sad) I have to point out that chatting up strangers isn't illegal. It's what makes life special! Talk to someone today! Anyone!

4 MOVE ABROAD

Has it ever been your dream to live in a different city or even a different country? Do you wish to be considered a local in more than just one place? From my personal experience, turning a new city into a home is one of the most rewarding things you can do. If you move somewhere new, one day – maybe after a year or two – you'll suddenly realize while walking down the street, you know exactly where to go and how to get around. Realizing what you've accomplished and how you can do things without thinking too much will most certainly fill you with pride! This very tiny moment will be your ultimate proof of independence!

When you move to a new city or country, you'll have to start building a life from scratch. There are cities that make arriving easy, and others that make it feel hard. As someone who has moved somewhere new several times during their adult life, I can only say, don't expect to feel welcome and settled from day one. Give it time!

Moving, even besides the bureaucratic hurdles, is challenging. If you move to a hip place where a lot of people seem to be coming (and leaving) every day, such as Berlin or New York, chances are the rent won't be cheap, but it'll be relatively easy to meet new people. Everyone's looking, not just for places, but also for friends! If you move somewhere that's not on one of the countless lists of trendy cities, such as Eindhoven or Salzburg, you might find it easier to find a nice, affordable apartment in a good location, but it might be more difficult to make friends since people already have their established social circles. Moving somewhere new is a guaranteed way to gain self-confidence and learn to trust your abilities, but also push your boundaries. If you're a freelancer, it's in your hands to challenge yourself. And if challenging yourself means spending time somewhere new for a couple of months, you should most certainly do that!

When you first put down your suitcase in a new place, you might be far away from feeling at home. What makes home a home are the people you're surrounded by. They are what will make you feel welcome and connected. The challenge is finding the good ones!

Coworking spaces are great to meet people. Most offer a trial day, so don't hesitate to shop around until you find a community you feel you can and want to become a part of. You can also look for groups on Facebook, meetup.com, and couchsurfing.com to find people for various activities. I'd also recommend finding your local Creative Mornings chapter, a monthly talk dedicated to a theme with free breakfast, and chat up people there.

Once you find some people you like, once you have your favorite café, some restaurants and parks, and once you learn to love the quirkiness of your new surrounding, you'll feel more accomplished. Making a place feel home from scratch makes you overcome many fears. You'll be busy settling and won't even notice all the side effects your move will have on you that you'll benefit from in the long run.

Independently of where you are in life, moving away won't get easier. If you feel like you'd like to spend some time abroad, it might be best to look for a project to give your journey a purpose; simply to help justify your decision. Escape the City, for example, is a platform that connects people with interesting projects around the world. You could decide to spend some time volunteering, or you could try to work in an office abroad, but within your branch to expand your horizons and learn something new.

All in all, to make moving a pleasant experience requires a healthy amount of courage, some curiosity, and a bit of money on the side. If you've never lived away from home, why not give it a try for two, three, or four months? I promise you won't look back one day and think moving to South Africa or Spain was a big mistake. You'll likely remember what you learned from living there!

EMBRACE EVERY DAY

You don't necessarily have to move abroad to enjoy the perks of travel. If you're a little bit like me, you have your routines and your preferred places, and you might also choose the same streets to walk through to get from A to B. You might be stuck in what you know and are familiar with.

Being an everyday traveler and embracing travel in your day-to-day means questioning your routines regularly and challenging the things you do and the way you do them. Being an everyday traveler means you won't ever accept doing things a certain way because you've always done them that way. Being an everyday traveler means you'll consciously seek out adventures and look for new places to explore, even if it means you'll take a ten-minute detour to get to work.

Given that stepping out of one's routine takes effort, you might have to consciously make space for exploration in your calendar. You might even want to go as far as making a jour fixe and dedicate a certain time weekly or monthly to your adventures. It's not unusual to need a prompt to explore. It's human to do things a certain way and continue to repeat endlessly. Thus, having a jour fixe might not seem very spontaneous; however, it might be the only way to regularly remind yourself you're falling into your old patterns. And you need to break them as to not get tired of your surroundings!

If you do things a certain way, why not think of alternatives? If you're a member of a coworking space, why not sign up for another coworking space for a month? If you go running each morning, why not run to a different attraction instead of running the same route? If you buy certain kinds of groceries from the same brand each day, why not grab the one lying right next to it instead? I believe the reason why we crave going on vacation so much is because it's the ultimate prompt to explore. Travel makes it easy to truly see because you don't know anything, so everything you do is exploration.

One of the most significant sentences anyone ever said to me came from my yoga teacher, Claas Hille, in Utrecht. Once, when I came to his lesson, it was right before the summer and I asked him whether he was planning to go somewhere for vacation. He laughed at me and said he didn't believe in the concept of a vacation. He believed that one should live their life in a way where there wouldn't be any need to take a vacation. Making the effort to make every day a (daring) adventure has been something I've been striving for since.

In your everyday, exploration and adventure are a conscious choice! When you think about it, you'll most likely realize there's enough to see in your city or region that you haven't explored yet. Just sit down with a friend and make a bucket list of all the places you always wanted to go, but never managed to. Then, make a pact to go together and set a date when you'll start!

The easiest way to attempt seeing your city with new eyes is by buying a travel guide. You don't even need to buy a mainstream travel guide. You can take the time and research alternative travel guides compiled by lifestyle and travel bloggers. Personally, I've been a long time user of the app Foursquare. There, I keep a running list of places I want to see one day. Whenever I have an hour or two to spare, I open the app, look for what's closest, and go. I might randomly end up having a cake at a café I haven't been to yet, or stroll through a park to see a statue I once randomly discovered on Instagram. Instagram is also how I've trained myself to look for beauty in the day-to-day. I believe that if you practice finding the good, you'll see it more often!

One thing is certain: you don't have to go on vacation to have new experiences. You just have to step up and make it your business to realize whatever you wish. Off you go!

*I*n a way, all the interviews you've already read are travel interviews, so what makes these three special for me to include them
in the travel section? I'd love for you to meet Kaitlyn Reed, Stephanie
Danforth, and Liz Wellington.

What I admire about Kaitlyn is that she's been living in Airbnbs
all around the world for several years. She found her home in her
boyfriend and together, they've lived all over the globe, moving their
carry-ons from door to door and country to country on a monthly
basis.

Stephanie has been a digital nomad for a couple of years. She
dropped out of school and decided to teach herself web and graphic
design in order to be able to move her work from the hospital and
into the cloud. Yes, she's a trained nurse! Steph doesn't get scared of
the things she doesn't know yet because she knows she's capable of
teaching herself just about anything.

And Liz, a writer and copy editor, is someone who's so good at making every day a real adventure. She doesn't hesitate to take the bus
across town to work in a new neighborhood for an afternoon. And
she doesn't fear traveling by herself, even though – and maybe also
because – she has a loving partner who supports and encourages her
to do the things that are important to her.

Here are the remaining three stories. Are you as sad as I am that you've
almost reached the final pages of this book?

KAITLYN REED

WORSHIP EVERYDAY
ADVENTURES; THE
SUPERMARKET CAN
BE ONE IF DONE
RIGHT!

What's been your educational and professional path?
I was a Journalism major with a minor in Photography. My professors warned me that print will eventually die, so that's when I decided to flip flop my studies and make Photography my major and Journalism my minor.

I graduated in 2012. Because they allow you to only start paying back your loan a year after graduation, it felt like I had a year where I didn't need to worry about it too much. I was able to save up some money during my studies, and my partner and I decided to go on a trip to Europe we thought would be for three months. In an attempt to save up, we sold all of the big things that wouldn't fit in my parent's garage. The trip truly changed our lives because when we got home for Christmas, we didn't feel like looking for a new place to live in Austin. We missed Europe a lot. Because my partner has his own company, he can set the rules for how he runs it. We enjoyed living through Airbnb and we thought we might just try and work from other parts of the world until we got tired of it. So far, we definitely haven't! When we first started traveling, the two of us were together for over two years. I still worked for a friend's company doing customer service. I did that for two years, and even though it was a remote job, I had to work regular work hours because I needed to be on the phone a lot. Depending on our time zone, I sometimes had to work in the middle of the night. Other times, I had to get up really early. It became tiring and I was frustrated about my situation, even though I enjoyed my teammates. To them, it was a complete surprise that I quit. I was the only member on the team really taking advantage of abroad travel. Even though everyone was remote, everyone had jobs and houses and loved ones with office jobs and only took weekend trips around America.

Given that we were told at uni that with a photography degree, we'd have to work out creative ways to make a living, I was used to the idea of project-based work. It was okay for me to leave a job without having a project lined up. I knew I'd eventually find another one, and for the time being, I had savings I could tap into.

Retrospectively, most of the projects I've worked on in the past few years started as something I was just really passionate about, or were doing for myself already. To give you an example: one thing I've been doing for a long time, more than six years actually, was RVSPing people to SXSW parties. During SXSW, there are more than 500 parties in Austin that one could attend. It's crazy, and a lot of work if you need to RVSP yourself! At first, I was just RVSPing for myself and a couple of friends, but then someone heard about me doing it and said they'd pay money if I did it for them. I set up a landing page where I explained what I did for a fee of $99 and companies, such as Soundcloud, Foursquare, and Nokia, paid me to RVSP their employees. People found so much value in my service that I just got more and more clients through word of mouth, and the business grew each year organically. Responding to all these events could take hours, so I just made everyone a personalized calendar, which saved them a lot of hassle.

Because of my partner's company, Sched.org, an event scheduling app, we've always gotten invited to a lot of different events. When you see such a variety of events, you start picking up on what's good, what works, and what doesn't work too well. It really inspired me to start an events experience agency. One of my favorite projects that I worked on was organizing pop-up events for Pinterest. It was another one of the projects that landed in my lap through a recommendation. The team at Pinterest was looking for someone who could organize three large events. Whenever companies need someone who's flexible about their location, they usually hire outside of their existing talent. The team at Pinterest had a lot of different ideas of what they wanted to do and they needed someone who could drive their ideas, find the right people, scout the right places, and coordinate everything that was necessary for these pop-ups to be successful. I ended up organizing a surprise dog park in Boston, an outside movie theatre in Philadelphia, and then I also helped redecorate a girl's dorm room to showcase what Pinterest is good for and how to turn inspirational pinboards into real life results.

All in all, I've just been very lucky with people finding my passion projects worth their money. And, of course, I've also been lucky having a partner that makes me push myself every single day. He might probably say the same thing. I think we both definitely realize how lucky we are we found support in each other and that we have found work that allows us this kind of lifestyle.

How is your business set up?
My most recent project is Workcation Club. A lot of people have been asking my partner how he's managed to book all these great houses all around the world to gather Sched's remote team for collaborative work sessions, team trips, brainstorming sessions, or just purely for relaxation. He always responded that I take care of all the organizing. After hearing people asking him over and over again about how he does it, I realized there was business potential. Workcation Club isn't just a service for teams that already work remotely, but also for companies that want to take their teams on a retreat to have a more focused time somewhere outside their regular base. I charge a fixed fee and take care of all the booking and even provide an itinerary so you know what you could do with your team. My lifestyle really is my best business card. Because it's so easy for people to see what I do, they trust me that I'll do a good job doing it for them as well.

How would you describe your attitude towards travel?

One could say that my partner and I have been on a life experiment trying to understand what makes a place feel like home. Wherever we go, we stay at least a month or two and really try to live like locals. We find a grocery store and a coffee shop, and build a little routine. It makes a difference if you go to the same coffee shop for more than a week and get to know the barista and regulars there. Once our time at an Airbnb is almost over, we pack our bags and do it all over again somewhere else. It's often hard to decide where to go next. We're quite spontaneous. Sometimes, we have events we need to attend and we have a date and a place blocked in our calendars. In the meantime, we just pick a place based on the lifestyle we feel like having next. Sometimes, we want to stay in a cabin somewhere in the Alps, other times, we prefer to be somewhere near a beach, and sometimes, we're up for a bit of city life. We pick the dates we want, a price range, and just zoom out on an entire country or region of the world. There are a lot of areas where Airbnb isn't as well-known just yet, so in those places choices are limited, which makes it easier to pick a place.

When you make new countries your home, even if it's just for a limited period of time, a walk to the grocery store suddenly turns into an adventure. I really don't mind doing errands in all these different places because they help break up the day. I like doing the simple things; cleaning the house and going to the grocery store. It gives me comfort to be able to create a routine, maybe because I know it's only for a short time and that's why I savor it so much.

Because our lifestyle is based on diversity, we enjoy having routines a lot. They make us feel comfortable. Eventually, we want to find somewhere we can settle down in. What we're seeking is a home. We pick up little things here and there about what we'd like our future home and our community to look like. We now know what sort kitchen table we want and we know we can't live without a garbage disposal. We've experienced these things and have seen their value. We also know that in our future home, the people in our community have to be warm and inviting, like in Bali or Greece. It's funny that when you talk to people about their favorite places, they often say how beautiful the landscape is. Hardly ever do people tell you how beautiful the people are. We had that experience in Greece. Everybody always praised the beauty of the country, but no one ever mentioned the kindness of the people. Greeks are some of the most hospitable, welcoming, and kind people we've met. That's what we look for when traveling. Wherever we decide to settle one day, the people will have to be nice. Over time, we've made a lot of friends in different places, and with the people we like the most, we love to stay in touch through Facebook, Swarm, or Instagram. It's really great when you meet the people you've connected with somewhere else in the world.

Most people travel to places to see nature. We travel to get to know people. Since we don't have a home, we have to make one, and the most important part of a home is the community, so wherever we go, we create one.

I feel very fortunate to experience so many different cultures. It really opened my eyes and it also made me appreciate a lot of things we consider normal in the US. I appreciate the different cultures and religions. Traveling just makes you aware there isn't just one culture or one religion that's right. I once read a story about an elephant that touched me deeply. It was about blind men of different religions. Each one of them touched an elephant and each one of them thought they knew what an elephant looked like, even though they all only got a part of the story. It was a story that made me realize that none of us are 100% right and that we need to collaborate and talk to get the full picture. I remember reading this story in a café in Bali and just crying over it.

Over the years, we've seen many different celebrations of cultures. For example, it's beautiful that Hindu Buddhists celebrate something every single day, whether it's a beautiful flower or a scent. It's incredible to see how people celebrate life and karma and how they're just generously kind to everyone.

How did you start implementing work into your life after you went nomadic?

My partner's company has always been remote, so I knew that if we wanted to keep traveling, I had to figure out how I'd make money on the road. At first, I had the job at AgentPronto.com, where we matched up people trying to sell or buy a home with the top realtors in the city. After I quit that, I had enough money saved not to feel too pressured. I knew a project would come along eventually. I guess my partner helped me gather courage. He'd say to me over and over again that nobody should be unhappy with their job. His work brings him so much joy and it really inspired me not to settle for just any project. He'd often go to a coffee shop straight after waking up to get as much done as possible, and that always encouraged me to follow his lead. I've started a lot of fun projects, such as PhotoYolo.com or MyLoveLetterToYou.com.

How do you communicate your approach to work and travel to your clients?

Our lifestyle has been what inspired me to create Workcation Club, so the digital nomad lifestyle is also the proof of concept for my business. In other words, Workcation Club is the professional, monetized version of my life.

What's your process to feel at home in each new place you move to for such short time?

Whenever we move to a new place, it takes us about a week to feel settled. A week is roughly the time we need to find a routine, a grocery store, and a coffee shop. Over time, I've reorganized a lot of kitchens. Often, it doesn't make much sense how people set them up. You notice that no one lives in the houses that are up for long-term rental, so it doesn't even cross their minds to organize the contents in the kitchen or to have certain utensils. I like to be in a place that feels like home that's comfortable for us to cook in. We love farmers markets and the diversity of different cuisines. In

Europe, the farmers markets are exceptional, so there, we eat a lot of vegetables. In Asia, on the other hand, supermarkets are very expensive, so we mostly eat out. Restaurants are much cheaper there. Because not every kitchen we move into has the same appliances, we change our set of recipes a lot. One place might have an oven and we'd eat a lot of veggies, and the next apartment comes without an oven and we need to cook something completely different. Even though it takes about three days after our arrival to unpack our laptops, we always check the wifi first. Having great wifi is essential for us to be able to work comfortably. Once our laptops are out, that's when real life starts. When we have about a week left in a city, we start looking for a new place. Sometimes, we go back to where we liked the most. We've gone to Japan a couple of times, Bali, and we've really fallen in love with the Netherlands. I know that our wanderlust won't slow down anytime soon, so if we really miss a place, we'll go back. I've talked a lot about routines and work, but I also believe that you should always make sure there's at least one thing outside of work you look forward to every day. Set a time when you'll close your laptop and go outside. It depends on where we are, but we'll always make sure that we at least catch the sunset.

How does it work out financially for you?

I've always had enough projects come my way that I'll never run out of money. But working on projects here and there definitely puts me on a budget. I do think about every expense and if it's necessary. I believe there's always a choice; will you spend the money on an expensive dinner, or will the money go towards your next plane ticket?

We live quite frugally. My partner is more outgoing and he loves to soak in the local cuisine and drinks. He has a consistent income; it's how he's built his business model, so it's mostly me who needs to think about how much money I have and how far it will go until the next project comes around. Not having a stable income definitely makes you want to stay at home more, watch a movie, and cook your own meal instead of dining in a restaurant and going to the movies afterwards. Occasionally, we'll do that, but given that our way to travel is slow and we try to treat a lot of the places where we're staying like home, we don't go out every night. No local would ever do that!

Social media often makes people believe we're on vacation all the time, but that's definitely not true because we both work a lot. We've just chosen not to spend rent in an expensive city like Austin. In Austin, we used to pay $1,000 for rent, so that's become our limit for how much we want to pay in other places. We know that some places will cost us more than that, but usually we try to find something cheaper. The smallest apartment we've had so far with that budget was in Paris. In Bali, we got a three bedroom house with a daily maid service, a pool, and a lawn guy for the same amount of money. It really depends on what you want, what lifestyle you want, and even the tiniest apartment can be a lot of fun. I have very fond memories of our time in Paris, not just because it was my very first time in Europe, but I loved cooking our dinner at a small burner and sitting side by side on a couch because that's all there was. It was charming not to have too much money and just be so aware of what an adventure we were on.

When booking a place with our budget in mind, we pay special attention to how good the kitchen looks, if there's a big table for us to work at, and we make sure the wifi is fast enough. I usually ask the hosts to check their wifi by sending them to speedtest.net. However, lately I started asking if the wifi is strong enough to stream Netflix and if they say yes, then I know the wifi will work for us. We're very upfront about how much the speed of their internet matters to us, and if it isn't, we ask if we can upgrade to a faster one. So far, it's worked.

How do you budget for your travels?

It's a misconception that our lifestyle is more expensive. Because we live like locals and because we don't buy things for our home or clothes (we can't bring more with us than what we can carry), we don't have a lot of the spendings you might have if you live in one place. Our housing costs us usually anything between $1,000 and $2,000. That already includes all the bills. Then, we only need money for food, which is an expense we'd have everywhere else too. We collect miles with our credit cards and use them for long-haul flights, and we depend on cheap airline fares when we travel between countries in Europe or Asia.

Luckily, we've never been sick on the road, but once, my partner's co-worker's wife wasn't feeling well while we were on one of our Workcations and she needed to go to the hospital. The bill ended up being something like $30. For all the treatments she got, that would've cost thousands of dollars in the US. We've never been close to zero in our bank accounts, so we aren't too worried about anything going wrong. We can also always go home and stay with our parents should anything dramatic change in our lives.

What's something you'd recommend to others who want to travel the way you do?
I'd say to slow down. Many people are always trying to see everything in a very short period of time. It might have something to do with our culture; how we've been raised. I don't think it's important to go to Paris only to see the Eiffel Tower. I really think it's far more important to get to know the culture behind it. Ask who built the Eiffel Tower and why, and learn why the people of Paris hated it at first before it became symbolic. Those are the things that will change the way you think. It's not just about seeing the structure of the Eiffel Tower and climbing to the top. It's really about understanding its meaning.

Kaitlyn Reed on
Web: workcation.club
Instagram: @kaitlynreed

STEPHANIE DANFORTH

NEVER

STOP LEARNING!

What's been your educational and professional path?

I went to school for nursing in Texas, but never actually finished. My husband and I got married when we were about 19 and we began traveling shortly after. It was a little serendipitous because at first, we went on a few small trips around the US and Europe. However, we liked it so much, we decided to just keep traveling! For me, it was a decision between going back to school and doing the thing you're supposed to do, or simply living in the present and finding ways to make it work. I decided for the latter.

Our journey to becoming location independent wasn't a typical one. We moved into a campervan to gain flexibility while living in Austin, which was about a year after we got married. I wasn't really on board at first. Living without a proper toilet wasn't necessarily on my agenda. It's adventurous though, for sure! Looking back, we had some incredible experiences and simply made it work. Then, while we were still living in the van, we decided to go on a trip to Europe for one month. We wanted to see if it was doable for us to manage the time difference and work remotely. It worked, so we decided to sell our campervan and travel full-time!

We were very lucky because my husband always had a job that allowed him to work remotely. However, in the beginning, we lived on a shoestring because I wasn't earning anything. When we lived in our campervan, I created jewelry that I sold on Etsy. I had found designs on Pinterest and thought to myself I could make it myself, and so I did. Etsy was a good outlet and helped me make some money. Previously, I worked as a barista to make ends meet while I was still in school. Naturally, when we then left the US, I didn't have a job and I most certainly couldn't travel around with a big suitcase filled with jewelry. My husband was the driving force behind this adventure. Because I didn't work or study when we left the US, I had a lot of time to figure things out. We left with just a backpack each and our plan was to explore different destinations. I couldn't do what I did before and I also couldn't work at a coffee shop. It quickly became clear I needed to find something I could do while on the road. I found an online course and some free resources and started learning more about web design. Because web design is so visual, I felt I would be good at it.

With the basic knowledge I had, I started applying for assignments through Elance, which later became Upwork. My style's always been very feminine and minimalist, which is probably why my designs attract predominantly a female audience. To get started, I created a couple of personal projects for me to be able to demonstrate the quality of my work and showcase my style. With or without work experience, you can always make up projects to show what you're capable of!

Becoming successful on Upwork requires persistence. It took a while to figure out how the platform works. It's a highly competitive environment, so while I was teaching myself more about design, I also had to teach myself how to communicate with potential clients. It can take a lot of time until you land your first client! Sometimes, I'd hear back from people and still not get the job. But really, just hearing back from them at all showed me I was moving in the right direction. I liked figuring out different ways to approach people, so I just kept hammering on it. I kept applying for up to three hours every day just because I had nothing better to do, and then kept refining how I applied for assignments via Upwork.

Once I got some traction and the first few people started working with me, it sort of snowballed and I was getting more and more assignments. That took five or six months of continuous applying from what I remember. Having reviews on these sort of platforms really matters. You'll definitely have to start below what you'd usually ask for your work, but once you have good reviews, you can increase your prices!

How is your business set up?

I recently set up a boutique branding studio, Mint Made, but I've made the majority of my income through Fiverr. It was tough at the beginning, mostly because Fiverr gives you the feeling of underselling yourself because you can only charge $5 at first. It was really daunting for my ego, but once I figured out how the platform works, it ended up paying quite well. I think I got a bit lucky and was just in the right place at the right time with the niche I'm in on Fiverr! It changes the game on any platform once you get good reviews! You can start raising prices, as I did with my logo design packages that I offer on Fiverr. Instead of charging $5, I'm now able to charge $25 per order and luckily, I have about 20 to 50 outstanding orders at any given time. Seeing that also made me realize that I might be able to find clients who might want to work on much bigger projects. That's why I founded Mint Made Studio!

My husband and I both have location independent careers, which gives us the freedom to return to the US without worrying about not having work because we can bring our jobs with us.

When we decided to sell our van, it all became very real. Suddenly, we were on the road and there was nowhere to go back to. It's emotional to let go of something that gives you the feeling of security. You can go from Airbnb to Airbnb, but it's still not your home. Having a place that feels like home is comforting and after a little while, you really miss it. Also, after being digital nomads for a few years, settling feels like the most adventurous thing to us. I've gone back and forth on that. There are times where it's really nice to see what others are up to on Facebook and be very content with where you are yourself, but then there are times where it makes you feel like you want to be there with them. It's definitely something very interesting to me that even when you have the life everyone supposedly wants, you still know others also have something you really crave.

How would you describe your attitude towards travel?

Typically, we spend a month in each place. Sometimes, we spice things up and spend a week or just a weekend somewhere else, just like everyone who lives in a stable location. It's definitely a slow kind of travel. We've been on the road for a few years and have traveled to a lot of different countries. We don't have a count we want to hit. For us, it's no longer about seeing more, but about going to places to see the people we want to spend time with.

In the past two years, we've met a lot of like-minded people and because it can get lonely if you travel as a couple, we try to align our travel plans with the plans of people we like to spend time with. There's something about having a consistent community! You take it for granted if you have a home, but being on the road teaches you how special it is! I've definitely gone through phases of loving my lifestyle, but then also hating it. Once you've been on the road for awhile, you suddenly realize how great it is to have a consistent group of friends. Of course, at the beginning it's very exciting to meet all these new wonderful people, but at some point, you crave having more consistent relationships and seeing people you like regularly. If, on the other hand, we go somewhere where we don't know anyone, we make sure to tap into the local community quickly. Heading to a local coworking space or looking up meetup. com has worked the best for us!

How did you start implementing travel into your work life after you went freelance?

For me, it's definitely been the other way around. Our very first trip was a traditional backpacking trip. What was different to others is that even during that time, my husband was still working. We had to stop somewhere every day and spend three to four hours in a café or a hostel that had wifi for him to get work done. I would usually read a book while he worked. That was before we decided to do this long-term and I began teaching myself new skills to eventually find work. The digital nomad scene is deeply focused on work, productivity, and earning money. Everyone's trying to figure out how they can make a living while traveling long-term, so you get infected. There have been many books written about how to keep up in a digital nomad lifestyle. The truth is that it takes an enormous amount of time to build up, even to a degree where you might forget you're in a different country and should take the time to explore.

While there are many hotspots where you can find other nomads to surround yourself with, I like to get outside the bubble a bit. Now that I'm used to the lifestyle and feel a bit more "stable," I find that when I travel, I do so for travel's sake. Meaning that if I'm checking out somewhere new, it's not likely to be digital nomad hotspot and I'm instead going on a "real" trip.

Having freelance work is one of the best things when it comes to managing a schedule and figuring out how to fit in time to travel because I can take time off almost whenever I want!

How do you communicate with your clients when you're in a different time zone?

I'm very upfront about where in the world I am when drafting a proposal for assignments. Given I've built up my business while traveling full-time, it's never been an issue for me. I've always worked on short-term, project-based assignments that enabled me to be flexible. In cases when it matters and I need to communicate with a client regularly, I just say which times of the day I'll be online and available. Most people are flexible and if someone isn't, then they're just not the right client for me. It's your life, you have to make it work to meet your needs! I have friends who work for US clients and adapt to the US nine-to-five, even if it means they work from 9pm until 5am. That just wouldn't be something I'd be willing to do. I really believe the more clear you are about how you work with people, the easier it will be to find a way that works for both parties.

Being self-employed, how do you balance your work life?
Being a part of the digital nomad community, it's easy to just never stop working. Everyone seems so disciplined and are always hustling! It's tricky to structure your own work day when you're self-employed and have an endless list of personal projects you want to work on and things you want to accomplish. I try to write down a list with tasks that I want to accomplish each day. A big learning for me was to learn how to be easy on myself, realizing that things will take care of themselves and there's usually enough money in the bank account, so there really is no reason to be stressing out. I have a list where I break the tasks down I need to work on, from personal to client projects. It's things like working on my website, finding leads, or sending out proposals. I also use Trello to manage projects.

At the beginning, I adapted my schedule to catch people in Europe and the US during their work hours. Asia is roughly twelve hours ahead of the US, and about six to eight hours ahead of Europe, so I'd be up early to catch people or I'd stay up really late. However, I'm not an early bird, so it was quite hard for me to find a suitable routine. Now, I try to work regular hours, 9am until 5pm, wherever I am. I work in small chunks and take little breaks. I've reduced meetings or schedule them in a way so they're not spread throughout the day. As a freelancer, it's easy to just keep working because of the lack of all the outside impulses, so one really has to make a conscious effort to take breaks, to close the laptop, and do something else. Even on the road, you should still take time to work out or cycle somewhere for a bit. Because I've decided to work regular hours, I try to go to places that I want to see on the weekends or after dinner. Occasionally, we'd take short trips to other places. It's really not that different from people who live in one location.

Depending on the day, I'd usually wake up between 8–9am. I don't use an alarm clock anymore, so it depends on how the day before went and when I went to bed. Then, I get ready and head to a coffee shop. Sometimes, we'd work from the Airbnb and then head out for lunch and work in a café afterwards. Depending on the country, we mostly eat out for lunch and then eat in for dinner. We try to finish between 5–6pm. I have a tendency to just stick to my laptop, so I have to be very conscious about implementing weekends in my schedule. Occasionally, I also take an extra day off. Especially if we're in Asia, we'd take Monday off because it's still Sunday back in the US. I know of a lot of people who don't do weekends or sometimes only take half a day off, but as for myself, I know that I couldn't do it. I also don't want to do it. There's so much to see, so it's about consciously managing your time.

How does it work out financially for you?

At the beginning, my husband and I only had his income. At that time, we lived off maybe $2,000 a month, which was very modest but it taught us how to keep our expenses in check. Now, it might be somewhere between $3,000 to $4,000. Ideally, we'd like to earn about $6,000–$10,000 a month. Even though we could very comfortably live off of both our incomes, we still live off just his salary and we try to save my income. It's become a thing for us to conserve money and try to plan for what the future might hold.

Luckily, we're on the same page when it comes to money. There's no separation between his and my money. There's a mutual understanding of the other person's needs. However, given that we live out of our backpacks, it's not that we'd ever buy anything big. We just replace things when needed. When we first started traveling, it was a planned trip for a couple of weeks. We didn't have a big chunk of money saved up because we expected to come back. Also, my husband worked throughout that trip, so we had access to a fixed income. Our safety cushion was mostly that we still had our van in the US we could return any time. While we've rarely gotten that close to a zero in our bank account, we've definitely been in a couple of situations where we've spent money to have some friends come out and then realized we hadn't gotten paid for some of our invoices and needed to keep our spendings lower than usual. It's usually just a cash flow issue, especially with me freelancing! The good thing with being highly rated on platforms, such as Upwork or Etsy, is that you can go back to them at any time if you really need to. If we ran out of money in Europe, we'd probably make work our priority and just work as hard as we could to get our finances up again.

Sometimes, we drain our bank account for flights, but then we also know that we want to keep pouring money into our investment fund, which we do religiously, even during the slower months. It helps that life outside of the US has been much cheaper for us. Additionally, both of us work with clients in the US, so that's why at the end of the month, there's always something left to save. We earn enough to feel comfortable, however, we both look beyond that. We'd like to get more into investing. In the long-term, we'd love to be able to live off of the returns of our investments and retire early.

How do you budget for your travels?
I wouldn't say we do. With places where we've been before, we know how much we're likely to spend, so it's not that we set a budget. We really like Chiang Mai, Thailand, because so many great people are coming through there and it's a good place to get work done, so that's one of the places where we spend a lot of time. Often, we coordinate with people via WhatsApp or Facebook and really try to get together again. When we go somewhere we haven't been before, we usually ask on forums, such as NomadList, to feel it out. But at the end of the day, we spend about the same amount of money wherever we are. I guess it's mostly about having habits that let you estimate your overall spendings. To give you an example, when we went to Budapest, eating out isn't as common and

it's more expensive than in other places. In that case, we'd mostly go grocery shopping instead and cook ourselves. But in Thailand, eating out is the norm, so that's what we do when we're there and it's very affordable.

Regarding accommodation, when you live in a city, you often forget that rent is much cheaper in the countryside or smaller towns. We don't spend time in places like New York, Paris, or London, so we're able to budget between $600 and $1,000 for accommodations. That would be hard to come by in almost any big city! Also, when we stay with friends, which is something we've done more and more lately, the costs are even cheaper because we split the rent. The only extra expense we have are the flights we take from place to place, but given we're US citizens, we can play the credit card game, so we have a ton of miles. We use them for long-haul flights and then book cheaper airlines to get around Europe or Asia.

What's something you'd recommend to others who want to travel the way you do?

My personal recommendation would be to just try it. Book a trip somewhere, but then think of a personal project that you could pursue during that time to see if it's something you can see yourself doing full-time. Just use the time well. You don't need to plan out what you buy and bring with you. That's secondary. What I believe is important is to see if you actually enjoy working on the road.

If, financially, you aren't in a place to travel full-time just yet, think of how you can expand your personal project into something that will eventually make you money. That's something you can do while you're still employed!

Stephanie Danforth on
Web: mintmade.co
Instagram: @steph_danforth

LIZ WELLINGTON

TREAT YOURSELF,
DRINK TEA AT THAT
FANCY HOTEL YOU
ALWAYS WANTED TO SEE

What's been your educational and professional path?
As a young girl, I completely immersed myself in stories, especially historical fiction. I realized I wanted to be a writer while attending a small liberal arts college where I gained a strong footing in the humanities before declaring a major in history.

I always loved history because it helped me make sense of a very fragile, chaotic world. It gave me the wisdom to answer the question, "How did we get here?" You may wonder why I didn't study literature. It was such a beloved part of my life, I didn't want to suck the joy out of it. Instead, I took a job at an independent bookshop and read voraciously.

My goal was to be a writer, but I didn't know how that would happen for a long time. I graduated during the recession – I couldn't get a full-time job and I didn't want to be a starving artist. The awful job market actually empowered me to get creative about how to make a living. Eventually, I bought a one-way ticket to France and got a TEFL certification in teaching English as a foreign language. I worked under the table for an eclectic Welshman at a language camp near Nimes. I worked 24/7 at the camp for a week or two, and then I would use that money to travel during the off periods. In between, I stayed with a friend in Montpellier, sleeping on a pallet on her kitchen floor. It wasn't romantic, but I loved immersing myself in the culture. During that time, I straddled both languages – English and French – and learned a lot about myself, like how resilient I was, and that doors open when you trust your instincts.

After working at a study abroad program in Nice that summer, I needed to come back for visa reasons. I found a job at a small, independent bookshop on Nantucket, and began working for a literacy program in the elementary school. Nantucket is 30 miles off of Cape Cod, a true small town and a beautiful island, and I savored my time there as much as I did in France. I made my way to Boston in 2012 and took a job in higher education, working for some of the brightest minds in academia. I found a pattern: I was doing everything that brought me close to writing without actually doing it. Instead, I was selling books, teaching English, and assisting academics. I made the leap to freelancing at the time when content marketing started taking off, and the synchronicity lined up perfectly for me. Even though my path is winding, cultural exploration and writing have always been the guide.

How is your business set up?
When I first started freelancing full-time, I wrote across a lot of different topics and areas. It was kind of like eating at a buffet; I tried a lot of things to see what I liked. Now, I'm more selective. I prefer to work with kind, flexible, and supportive clients, so that's a big part of the selection process.

I primarily write about creating a life and a career you love for a millennial audience. Within that large umbrella, most of my client work revolves around writing about the intersection of creativity, business, and fulfillment. A lot of projects have also given me insight into cutting-edge research on management, which was an unexpected gift — it feels like getting an MBA without the price tag. I structure my business so I have five to six big clients because I don't want any of my projects to account for more than 25% of my income. Some of my work is ghostwritten. I write an article through the unique lens of the company, and it's published under the name of their CEO or leader in a magazine, like *Inc.* or *Fast Company*. Ironically, ghostwriting helped me find my own voice by taking the pressure off. Articles I publish under my name often draw on my experiences as a solopreneur, creative, and freelancer; I really like writing about those topics from a personal perspective. In content marketing, these companies want to be thought leaders in their field and gain traction with prospects. Some hire in-house marketers to design the strategy and content, but they usually need help. They often give me a topic or a loose goal and I define the specifics from there. But, sometimes, I'm lucky and get an outline! I'm a big believer that strong freelancer relationships are an asset to the company. Because I'm outside of the work culture, I'm closer to the audience and bring a unique perspective to the conversation.

That said, a lot of my work is research. I allow what I find to guide the content, and that's where my history major comes into play. My clients hire me because I deliver well-researched articles and maintain an integrity that goes beyond click-bait. I'm grateful that I've gained enough traction so the vast majority of my work comes through referrals. I have warm relationships with my clients and other marketers in my community; I'm grateful they keep an open mind and recommend me on a weekly basis. At the beginning, I tried to turn over a high volume of articles. A lot of outlets pay around $100 for an average 1000 word article, but over time, I've raised my rates successfully. I try to balance client work with personal projects – I've published editorial work in *Travel & Leisure*, *The Charlotte Observer*, *The Week*, and *Misadventures Magazine*. My hope is to spend more time on these projects, writing about my personal journey and love of travel.

How would you describe your attitude towards travel?

This may sound odd, but I like to travel the way I live. I love to explore a culture and I'm a bit of a homebody, so I set up a comfortable base. I'm not a huge fan of hostels. I've always met wonderful people at them, but I always feel ungrounded and disconnected from the community I'm visiting. I prefer to mix it up, visit everyday places like coffee shops, and tourist-worthy spots like museums and parks.

When I travel, I create more internal space to be present with my experience and the landscapes I'm immersed in. I consider myself a pretty relaxed traveler. As much as I love exploring, I don't like to go home exhausted. Whenever possible, I walk everywhere. And most importantly, I eat my way through wherever I am.

To get to know different places, I try not to travel during the busier seasons and choose to stay in neighborhoods that aren't touristy. I recommend EatThisPoem.com for literary buffs who enjoy a beautiful meal and lovely independent bookshops. I also trust the travel guides on Grace Bonney's DesignSponge.com and always look at *On The Grid*. I keep an informal list of places I would love to visit. I take a lot of day trips and enjoy exploring outside Boston. I fell in love with New England, and nothing makes me happier than discovering its nooks and crannies. Once a quarter, I try to make a bigger trip. I usually book an apartment or a room at a inn for close to a week, which shakes up my routine.

I have a wonderful partner who loves to travel, but I still like to venture out on my own. Traveling solo is something I've always done – it's not only a way for me to connect with different places; it's a way I reconnect with myself. My boyfriend loves that travel is an essential part of my personality, and it quite frankly feeds my soul. He's always up for hopping on board, but he's just as likely to drive me to the airport and support the adventures I initiate on my own. As a young woman, I've noticed that traveling solo makes it easy to connect with people. I can go sit at a bar of a restaurant and savor the experience. It's easy to strike up conversations, especially when people learn I'm a writer who loves a good meal. In that sense, being a woman opens doors. In another way, it requires strong boundaries. Just the other week, a man said to me, "I'm not trying to hit on you" while I was eating alone at a bar, and then he hit on me. In these cases, I'm as clear as possible.

When I take a working vacation, I leave the administrative work behind. I try to focus solely on writing and, when possible, my own projects rather than my clients'. I often turn on an OoO, even if I'm doing project-based work because it means I'm not accountable to email. I try to tackle those things before I set out on the trip.

How did you start implementing travel into your work life after you went freelance?

Travel has always been an essential part of how I choose my jobs. Teaching English in France, for example, was a way for me to be abroad while earning money. Now, the flexibility of being self-employed gives me the freedom to set my own schedule and explore, both at home and on the road.

At the beginning, I knew I needed to build a strong business model. I tried not to dig too deeply into my savings by traveling, and I spent a lot of energy getting my processes into place. I waited nine months to take my first big 10-day trip after I started freelancing full-time. Even then, though, I took a lot of weekend and day trips. Now, I try to spend one work day in a different part of town. After my morning routine (meditating for a bit and free writing), I'll hop in a taxi or a bus to explore a new neighborhood. I try to work from a coffee shop I've never been to before and enjoy a nice lunch in a new spot. I'm also a big fan of working in libraries and museums. The cultured atmosphere and beauty of the art and literature inspire me. I belong to a private library, The Athenaeum and the Museum of Fine Arts, both of which are dreamy. I love living in Boston partly because of the small New England towns in every direction. I've also taken a ride out to a small town or two to work, which is rejuvenating in a different way. These little efforts infuse me with energy. They fill up my writing too. It's a conscious choice I make because it brings the feeling of travel into my everyday.

No one actually tells you how challenging it is to carve out time for yourself when you're your own boss. It's so easy to postpone free time – or those lovely experiences – in favor of the grind. Even though I left a full-time job for more flexibility, I realized I needed to take myself out of the mental framework that's been instilled in me from the time I was a small child. My new goal is to have a very different relationship with "work." I want to it to be something fulfilling rather than draining. I'm trying to claim that – and the freedom to choose what my day-to-day looks like.

In other words, I needed to get comfortable making free time and travel a priority. I try to think ahead a little bit while leaving room for spontaneity. I pencil in trips and time off into my calendar, and work deadlines around that. I've become proactive about discussing deadlines and giving myself a buffer. By being transparent about what works for me, I've set up a positive relationship that serves both parties. A couple times, last-minute projects have come up when I'm preparing for a big trip. As painful as it was to turn away work and money, I had to learn to say "no." Doing a last-minute assignment might give you an extra thousand dollars or more, but it can also make it impossible to have the kind of trip you planned. It's a simple boundaries lesson I've learned.

To help create more opportunities to travel, I'm actually writing about my trips more often. I've also started building connections with clients in different regions and countries with the hopes of going to visit. That way, I can explore new places while collaborating with clients; it's a win-win!

How do you communicate to your clients you're not going to be available?

I always tell my clients a few weeks in advance that I'm taking time off. I don't do it over the phone because I prefer to have something in writing. I also make a note of my upcoming trip under my signature for the week leading up to the vacation. And as I mentioned, I turn on an OoO notification early to give myself space to wrap up projects and pack for the trip. Being proactive about deadlines – and giving myself more than enough time – ensures that I'm fair to my clients.

I allocate almost twice as much time on my schedule than I think I need to for each project. That's something I learned from Greg McKeown's amazing book, Essentialism. I've also learned the hard way to set deadlines pretty far out too. For short articles, I ask for two weeks, and for longer articles, I like to make it three to four. Of course, some of my clients shoot me an email, and I turn the assignment around within two days because I know their process. But if someone needs a project completed in a day or two and it's going to upend my day-to-day, I charge a rush fee of 20%. It makes it worthwhile to work a much longer day, and it keeps me from feeling resentful and burned out.

I also always try to hit all deadlines before I leave for a trip, even if it's a working vacation. I've had some nightmares with wifi failing in the exact wrong moment, and it's not worth the stress. I boarded a train in the UK planning to use the wifi to submit an article. I had to pay 20 pounds for the wifi, and I barely got a signal! Then the train broke down in the middle of nowhere, and I was stuck for a few hours. We all had to board a train with no seats, and I ended up squatting on my suitcase in the aisle for four hours. But that train had wifi, so I edited while being curled up on my suitcase. I was so stressed about getting to my friend in London, and I felt terrified about missing the deadline. It's just not an enjoyable way to travel.

I like to think that being intentional about my boundaries saves me from more moments like that and it also benefits the work I deliver. My ideas had space to percolate, and I had a chance to refine my words over time. I also want to say that I'm not a brain surgeon, and I can turn off my work emails while I'm on the road. No one is going to die if I'm not available. I really love my clients and I always try to be as communicative as possible. But given that I work in content marketing and journalism, it's highly unlikely any email that comes through is an emergency. Most of my clients say things like, "So sorry to bother you – I forgot! Have an AMAZING trip!" when they see my OoO.

Being self-employed, how do you balance your work life?

As a business owner, you're never really done. Your work can ooze and expand until it takes over everything. I could absolutely spend

14 hours a day working and still have stuff to do. But I would absolutely burn out that way too. For me, the past two years have been about making the internal shift to know that I'm enough and give myself permission to say "no" to things that don't serve me. You'll definitely have the lingering doubts like, "If I do a little bit more of this, my business will be so much better." In those moments, I look at my life holistically and try to say something nice to myself. In the end, you want to create a life that gives you room to get better if you feel sick, or travel when you want to take time off – no one will give that to you! You have to give it to yourself.

Thankfully, I've studied eastern cultures and religions since I was 16, and I'm trained in a practice called Reiki. It keeps that critical mindset in check. Because of my experiences meditating, I know when it's my ego; any sentence with a "should" is usually bullshit. Every morning, I try to cultivate some time to free write and meditate. It reprograms that voice in my head that says I'm not good enough and sets the foundation for a conscious day.

I follow Julia Cameron's "The Artist's Way," which is kind of like a 12-step program for creativity. Cameron is a proponent of free writing, or as she calls them, "The Morning Pages." It's my way to process what I'm moving through in life – it "un-gunks" my energy and often leads to wonderful ideas. I still do it on the weekends because I just love to write. Even if I won the lottery, I couldn't live without putting pen to paper. I usually "work" about 40 hours a week, although I try not to think about it as work. It's not always in the usual 9-to-5 timeframe. I think of some activities as putting fuel in my creative engine, and I try to make time for that. If there's something I want to do during the day, like getting a bunch of vegetables from the farmers market or having coffee with a friend, I remember that it serves my business too. Because I work from home, I usually end my day with a walk around my little park nearby. If I'm at a coffee shop or downtown, I walk back home. My favorite freelancer ritual, though, is really unusual. Once a week, I put on a silly rom-com movie and do my bookkeeping.

When you build your own business, it's vital to reflect on your values and needs. For me, fun and self-care are included in that, even though they go against the grain of the puritan work ethic I inherited. Sometimes, I feel that tension. I remember my doctor told me I needed to come in every week for a vitamin shot. My first reaction was, "There's no way! I can't take that time out." But what's the alternative? That I won't have any energy because I'm putting my work above my health? We really limit ourselves when we place more value on "doing."

One turning point for me was when I started seeing the different things on my to-do list as tasks. I learned to distinguish between being a consumer and a producer of content. I'm very discerning in what I write. I should be just as discerning in what I read, watch, and scroll through. Now, I try to respond to emails or tweets in bunches rather than when they come through (sometimes more successfully than others). The same goes for projects: I'm moving from being reactive to proactive, which is empowering. I really love taking ahold of my schedule. I don't think I could go back to a 9-to-5 for that reason. Working in a more meaningful way and according to my own calendar is just too cool. It affords a lot of flexibility.

But I realized early on that it's easy to get into the same "grind" even as a freelancer. In 2015, I charged lower rates. In order to make a good income, I had to put so much work out there that I really wore myself out. So, I made a monumental decision to let go of some my clients with a lot of notice. One by one, I approached each contact and explained I was raising my fees. Some accepted it, and others decided to part ways on really good terms.

I can't overemphasize how important negotiating is to a sound freelancer business model. I'm an introvert who tends to undervalue my work, so it's painful for me. While negotiating, I often have to write out a script because I can't get the words out otherwise. A couple times, I've been shaking with fear, but I know it's the right thing. For example, one client needed more extensive edits, which resulted in us going way over the word limit for a project, even though we adhered to the "two rounds" included in the contract. Because it exceeded my estimations (and took twice the time I thought it would), I told them I needed to be paid per word. That way, every word I went over the limit by, I still received compensation for. If someone values your work and values working with you, then they'll try to meet your needs. This one particular client met me halfway, and he's my highest paying client now.

I also try to follow some personal guides for choosing assignments. I ask myself three questions: Does it pay well? Is it going to bring meaning to my day or career? Will it be fun and easy? I accept work that meets at least two of the requirements.

How does it work out financially for you?

I'm very intentional about giving myself a salary as if I have a regular job. I have a business checking account, and every week, I cut myself a check from it that I put in my personal checking account. About every six months, I reevaluate my salary to see if I need to tweak it or give myself a raise. Once, I called my financial planner to say, "I have this extra money in my business account. Can I give myself a bonus!?" He laughed and said, "You're your own boss and can do whatever you want, but if you need a permission, tell me where to sign!" Luckily, I'm at the point now where I'm thinking about maximizing my impact and creating the kind of life I want. I hustled a lot that first year. I wrote up to five small articles a day. Two years in and I'm trying to figure out how to get into a rhythm that's sustainable in every way: financially, creatively, personally, and professionally.

I should also note that I'm religious about paying my quarterly taxes. Each time I cut myself a salary check, I add 30% to a special tax account. When that time rolls around, I'm ready to go, and there are no surprises. I also built an emergency fund that's pretty significant. I love to shop and go on wonderful adventures, but I don't touch that money. If I do things right, it will always be there, and I'll need it.

How do you budget for your travels?

I'm more conscious about how I allocate all of my assets – time, money, and energy – than I used to be. To me, money actually is energy; I want to put into experiences that are enriching for me.

Before I go, I jot down a rough budget, allocating a certain amount to each day, plus extra for when things go awry. It's so easy to run into a situation when your flight gets cancelled, you're jet-lagged, and all you want is a good book and a fancy meal. I want to be able to cushion those moments. I keep a rough track of my spending in a pocket-sized notebook, rounding up to the dollar (or other currencies). I'm also very thoughtful about expensing costs to my business. "Everything is copy," as Nora Ephron said, and my explorations often feed directly into creative projects. I highly recommend talking to your tax consultant and doing some research. You'll be surprised by all the hidden expenses that you can charge to the business.

Aside from expenses, I think money is really about priorities. As much as I love to travel, I need a comfortable place to come home to at night. I think that's the nature of being an introvert. As much as I want to be able to enjoy being in a hostel room with 10 other people, I know I hate it. I've heard from friends that I refined taste, and I think that's fair to say. I love to stay in beautiful boutique hotels, but I've also figured out how to have those luxurious experiences without the price tag. When I lived in France, I started having a cup of tea at the fanciest hotel in each town or city I visited. You know why? A cup of tea is never going to cost you that much, but the experience is pure bliss. I would spend an hour or two in their fanciest dining room or outdoor garden with a cup of tea and a good book, being served by gracious servers. That moment will rejuvenate even the weariest traveler. I also realized that lunch, instead of dinner, is ideal at fancy restaurants. They're much more affordable with the same high-level of experience and quality of food. Plus, the lack of formality and fussiness makes it more fun. Instead, dinners are low-key affairs pulled together from a trip to the local market.

There are some things that I don't spend money on that help keep my budget in check. I prefer bringing my own food to the airport. I don't drink, so the money I save on wine goes towards that fancy tea I mentioned. I'm also a big fan of Priceline.com's rental car bidding process and Hotel Tonight – it's amazing what a steal you can get. I pay for everything by credit card, and I love those points I collect for future travels.

What's something you'd recommend to others who want to travel the way you do?

Everyone has different comfort zones when it comes to travel. I have some friends who feel great about booking a one-way flight to a third world country without knowing where they're going to sleep that night. I'm not that girl. If I were to travel that way, I would be in a state of chaos and personal crisis. My biggest piece of advice is don't fight who you are and the way you want to travel. Trust your instincts because the world is a big place. You know what you'll enjoy! That said, dissolving fears and inching (or leaping) outside your comfort zone is a beautiful thing. My limits have absolutely been tested on the road, and I'm better for it. I know I'm resourceful, strong, and flexible, and that wisdom feels like a great gift.

With those two things in mind, give yourself permission to go. During college, I wanted to spend a summer in the UK, and I just couldn't find an internship. I now know I didn't need a "legitimate" reason to go. I had the money. I could've just went. If you want to go somewhere and you don't know why, give yourself permission and simply book the trip. You can go. It's okay!

Liz Wellington on
Web: lizwellington.com
Instagram: @liz_wellington

Do you have the courage to do any of these?

- *What's a dream destination you've always wanted to see? What's stopping you? How will you overcome that hurdle? (And how long will it take you?)*

- *What's your ten-step plan to take off for a month? What are you going to do to prepare?*

- *What do you fear? How can you break that fear? Google how to overcome that particular fear. Deal with it!*

- *Have you gone somewhere by yourself? Why not? Plan a trip somewhere for a week!*

- *Start talking to a stranger at the bus stop or at your favorite café. Either it will be weird or it will be fun. Either or, you'll have a good story to tell!*

- *Have you considered looking for a temporary project in a different city? Make it one of your goals for this year!*

- *What café or restaurant did you always want to go to in your city? Go this week!*

*I*t was in the late spring of 2016 when I first started thinking about what I'd like to write about as the next addition to the series of *Insightful Guides for Freelancers* I started publishing back in 2015. In July, I sent out the first interview requests for this book. I thought working, traveling, and taking time off might be interesting subjects fellow freelancers would enjoy reading. By December of 2016, I gathered and edited all of the interviews.

I need about seven hours to record, transcribe, and edit one interview. The beauty of this process is I get to fully immerse myself in someone else's thoughts. I find it therapeutic to slowly think through everything someone said in response to a question I had. When editing Becky's interview, I had to stop working on it for a while. I had tears rolling down my cheeks. Her story was intense and resonated with me so much. Having had such a strong reaction to what was about to become a part of this book, it was clear I didn't want to produce just another lifestyle book. I wanted to publish a book that, even though it didn't have just one single message, would encourage you to ponder about your life, your values, and the opportunities life presents to you.

When I started writing the accompanying chapters – something I always do after I've conducted and edited all of the interviews – I didn't quite know what this book would turn out to become. I wasn't sure what I was about to publish, even when I went live on Kickstarter. There was just so much on my mind and there were so many things I wanted to share with you that I needed to deeply think about it all. It hardly ever happens that I spend a year working on one single project. With *Work Trips and Road Trips*, it was different. Once I sat down to write, I immersed myself in my thoughts. I experienced a flow; a smooth, unbroken continuity of thoughts. With some chapters, they took forever to write, even though I was constantly writing. I also spent hours and hours walking up and down my apartment. I played a ridiculous amount of Battleship and Solitaire. I ironed. I retreated to reading. I listened to podcasts. I danced. And all while keeping my laptop open to add just one more thought, just one more paragraph. Then again, luckily, there were chapters where I sat up in bed in the morning and wrote what I had on my mind and in my heart within as little as 20 minutes. I never knew how the day would go. Sometimes, I'd finish multiple chapters in one day, and other times, I needed days and days to write just one page.

Over the years, I've spent a vast amount of time on the road and in between places. Whenever I sat at an airport, it became impossible for me to focus on anything besides life. How things happen. How we meet people. Who these people are and what impact they have (or had) on us. When I first set out to become a freelancer, it was for love, and I somehow managed to make a thing out of me being a freelancer and writing about it. Unfortunately, the love passed, but writing has turned into a tool for me to steer my thoughts in various directions. As for this book and why you've read what you've read, I guess I wanted to embrace the idea that life is an incredible and ever-changing experience; a journey. Everything is constantly moving and shifting.

Having lived in five countries over the years – and if we're counting New York, then six – I've come to the conclusion that I'm the only constant in my life. Everyone I meet is a visitor, a passerby. Some people stay with me for longer, while others impact who I am and how I think in a snap, and then I move on again to have that sort of impact with someone else. **And that's okay.** Not everyone is meant to remain in our lives forever. Not everything we do is the right fit to remain endlessly. What might've been right yesterday might not be right today. Everything that happens, day after day, is pushing us in various directions. Different things, different events, require us to make different decisions; how we react and what we do with whatever life sets in front of us makes for a life that's either safe or boring, or makes for a life where you allow yourself to embrace even the worst moments as chances that might steer you in an unexpected direction. All of this is okay.

Had it not been for my relationship that turned into a long distance relationship before breaking apart fully, I wouldn't have written three books. I wouldn't be where I am today. I guess all of it, even if at times very painful, is wonderful as it is. Retrospectively, anyway. Some of the chapters you've read, I must admit, often felt like letters I was writing to myself. I wrote what I needed to read in that moment. During the process of writing, I discontinued a major client and booked a one-month vacation to do nothing but sit with myself and my thoughts on a beach. I've managed to emotionally let go of people I realized didn't want to be a priority to me (anymore). I've made small and big changes because I noticed that some of the things I was doing made me someone I didn't want to be. I also realized I was the only person who had the power to address the situation and adapt to things so I can be who I want to be. In your life, you're never the victim of your circumstances. You're always the main character who proactively turns circumstances into opportunities. You're the one who might tell a good story after drifting off on a slippery road.

Whenever I'd previously published texts, they were all very objective, and it's mostly been stories of other people I find admirable. With this book, which is much bigger than the others, I've most likely made something utterly selfish by making you read my inner thoughts and feelings, sharing my conclusions with you and making them the majority of *Work Trips and Road Trips*. You're invited to critique and challenge my opinions, of course. As a writer, it takes time until you get any sort of feedback. After you publish a book, you don't often hear what people were thinking while they read what you wrote, even though you see the sales, showing you how many people are interested in what you have to say and how many recommended your book. I'd really love if you'd write a review on Amazon, or even send me an email to hello@mkanokova.com. When publishing this third book, I knew it'd be much more personal than the previous two, so (as you might imagine) I'm also more nervous to have shared so much of me with you. I'd love to hear what you're up to, what you're thinking about, and what chances you've decided to take! I'd be incredibly touched if it was this book that gave you the nudge and helped you feel more courageous. If I helped even just one person realize that they can do something they might've had thought before wasn't for them, then that's all I could ask for.

Waving at you from the window of a train!

Love,
Monika

MONIKA KANOKOVA

Monika Kanokova gave up long ago on trying to define one single location as her home as much as she has given up on trying to find a job title that would summarize what she does. She has a fascination for city building and space design and its impact on people's lives. Her interest in social mobility has planted her interest in people's stories and their unique career paths. She specializes in technology-based communication solutions for them to have positive impact on people's relationships.

Legally, she's a freelance advertiser, but as she doesn't believe in classic advertising, her design-driven approach often leads to unconventional solutions.

She helps her clients build useful products. She optimizes customer relationships and communication by finding ways to add value to people's lives. She's worked with clients such as Kickstarter, Sched.org, SOS Kinderdorf or taliaYstudio.

Web: mkanokova.com
Twitter: @mkanokova
Email: hello@mkanokova.com

DIANA J. JOINER

Diana J. Joiner is an ecommerce copywriter within the fashion industry by day and a freelance editor and proofreader by night. After graduating with an English degree with a focus in teaching, she went abroad to Southeast Asia where she taught English in Thailand and traveled for seven months. Upon returning to the US, she decided to break away from her career path to pursue her true passions, writing and editing.

She was the editor for both *This Year Will Be Different* and *My Creative (Side) Business*, and continues to make her editing and writing career flourish on the side. Paying close attention to detail, strategically piecing words together to form beautifully-crafted sentences with depth and impact, and creating consistent fluidity is what she strives to do in every project she's involved in.

Words are her passion and her passion is words. And live music. And her dog, who gets more Instagram likes than she does.

Web: dianajoiner.com
Twitter: @joinerofwords
Email: djjoiner925@gmail.com

EWELINA DYMEK

Ewelina Dymek is a self-taught illustrator who lives in Poznan, Poland. Although she graduated with a diploma in English studies, she decided to follow her greatest passion, which is drawing, and therefore became a freelance illustrator. After graduation, she began another degree in graphic design, which turned out to be extremely handy in illustrating, as Ewelina combines both traditional and digital media in her work.

Apart from drawing and design, Ewelina's also interested in fashion. A few years ago, she discovered a way to combine these hobbies, thus becoming familiar with fashion illustration, for which she uses her imagination to interpret a particular designer's collection and work on fashion brand campaigns. Ewelina has always wanted to be a fashion illustrator, but with more commissions coming in from various companies not always related to fashion, she discovered how exciting it is to explore her horizons and work with creative people outside the fashion industry. She's always ready to face new drawing challenges and gain new experiences.

Web: ewelinadymek.com
Instagram: @ewelinadmk
Email: ewelinadmk@gmail.com

CHRISTIANE WALLNER-HAAS

Christiane Wallner-Haas is a digital graphic designer from top to toe. She became a computer nerd from the first moment she used one and created her own digital illustrations at age 11 – in Paint. When she was 13 years old, she developed her own websites, learned HTML and CSS, and made her own sparkly types and graphic designs with Gimp and Photoshop.

From that time on, she always strived to improve herself and used her leisure time to build her knowledge in all the digital creative fields. After her business school examination, she studied Multimedia Design and Graphic Design at *die Graphische* in Vienna. During her studies, she almost accidentally slipped into different freelance graphic design jobs for various creative agencies and small companies. She's been self-employed for more than five years and overly happy about working with so many wonderful and different clients.
She loves to work on beautiful things, embracing individuality, taking risks, and breaking rules to create simple but thoughtful designs.

Web: wallner-haas.net
Instagram: @cwhcreative
Email: christiane@wallner-haas.net

MEET THE
KICKSTARTER BACKERS
WHO MADE THIS PROJECT HAPPEN – THANK YOU!

For the third time, we were successfully funded on Kickstarter. Thank you so much, everyone, who's helped us make this project a reality! If you are looking for someone to help you realize a project, please reach out to someone from our community.

Also, keep tight as I am currently working to realize a lovely online space for us: wearesmartcreatives.com. It might be live by the time you read these lines!

Analytics

Aaron Cruz	AT	squarebracket.io

Arts

Katherine Reynolds	AU	katherineareynolds.com
Julia Benson-Slaughter	US	artofthefirebird.com
Jerolyn Crute Sackman	US	etsy.com/shop/PaperArboretum

Arts Therapy

Emery Hurst Mikel	US	creativelyhealing.com

Blogger

Lukas Havranek	AT	lukashavranek.com
Tina Gabriel	AT	ecovienna.at
Melina Royer	DE	vanilla-mind.de
Marina Tureczek	DE	glitterandtechno.com
Julia Schicho	AT	fanfarella.at
Marlies Kirchler	AT	toeprint.at
Martina Menzini	AT	spunkyrella.com
Anna Heuberger	AT	welovehandmade.at
Michaela Ambos	AT	cooloutfit.at

Branding

Andrada Udrea	RO	hardtask.ro

Business Strategy

Mike Lanner	AT	mikelanner.com
Anika Horn	US	anikahorn.com
Alexandra Abbrederis Simpson	AT	missbizzy.net
Lisa Langmantel	AT	lisalangmantel.at
Marie-Theres Riegler	DE	marietheresriegler.com
Steffen Staeuber	DE	createmeaning.com
Guillaume Vaslin-Reimann	AT	aboutguillaume.com

Communications

Goksen Caliskan	TR	gngc.biz
Philip Eggersgluess	DE	berlinlovesyou.com
Margot van der Krogt	NL	maeandmany.com
Severine Brichard-Rooney	FR	teleferic.life
Katharina Kamleitner	GB	watchmesee.com
Katharina Moser	AT	mosaik-agency.eu
Nadine Bieg	DE	nadinebieg.de
Matthias Parthesius	DE	parthesius.de

Community

Max Okonetschnikow	DE	weedmaps.com

Content Strategy

Sarah Krobath	AT	sattgetextet.com
Shannon Byrne	US	asongaday.co
Alexandra Prasch	AT	contentessa.at
Amro A Gebreel	GB	iamamro.co
Ina Eisenbeis	DE	eirys.com
Sarah Halbeisen	AT	look-what-i-made.com

Development

Jamie Milnes	GB	milnesdesign.com
André Kishimoto	BR	kishimoto.com.br

Digital Design

Sabine Ballata	AT	meshcreates.net
Sarper Erel	DK	sarper.se

Digital Strategy

Daniela Krautsack	AT	citiesnext.at
Paul Aaron	US	botanylabs.com

Education

Irina Solonkova	AT	didacticmediastudio.com

Event Services

Taylor McKnight	US	sched.com

Event Services

Tanja Vlcek	DE	goldenerhering.de

Fashion

Julia Müller	DE	annamariaangelika.com
Michael Pattison	DE	fusion-factory.de

Illustration

Raven Henderson	US	ArtfulDevo.com
Peter L Brown	US	thetoonist.com
Shonneri Herndon	US	shonneri.com

Interior Design

Andreas Radlinger	AT	pendulumshelf.com
Angelika Hinterbrandner	AT	ahinterbrandner.com

Marketing

Maximilian Eberl	AT	meberl.com
Dominik Berger	AT	attentionfox.com
Ashley McGregor Dey	US	geekandwander.com
Michael Jones	DE	eyeem.com/michael
Julia Kordes	DE	juliakordes.com
Sandra Bittmann	AT	contentadora.at
Klaus Heller	AT	klausheller.at
Christoph Richter	AT	about.me/piffie
Viktoria Egger	AT	august.at

Music

Jake Lewis	US	jakelewis.net

Photography

Tom Bates	GB	instagram.com/shotsonstone/
Natasha Ward	AU	natashaward.com.au
Kristina Satori	AT	kristinasatori.com
Kyle Studstill	US	composure.design
Cliff Kapatais	AT	pixelcoma.at
Ursula Schmitz	AT	ursulaschmitz.com
Christa Gaigg	AT	authentic.co.at
Roy Potterill	ZA	mobilemediamob.com
Petra Rautenstrauch	AT	rautenstrauch.at
Felipe Tofani	DE	fotostrasse.com
Gregor Hofbauer	AT	gregorhofbauer.photography

Product Strategy

Talia Radford	AT	taliaystudio.com

Project Management

Sarah E. Yost	US	bit.ly/SarahOnLinkedIn
Katarzyna Odrozek	DE	kasiaodrozek.com
Volker Göbbels	DE	technologyscout.net

Social Media

Tasha Turner	US	tasha-turner.com
Jeska Dzwigalski	US	jeska.org
Simone Schedl	AT	simonecrown.com

Sound

Laurent Mertens	BE	laurentmertens.com
Sarah Kickinger	AT	ravenandfinch.com

Styling

Sabine Reiter	AT	craft-up.com

Visual Design

Chris Cambell	GB	chriscambell.com
Pascal Tax	NL	emblend.nl
Jessica Ringelstein	DE	jringelstein.de
Marina Hauer	GB	apricitysolutions.co.uk
Anastasia Crosson	US	savvymediagal.com
Hazel O'Keeffe	DE	nuttymakes.ie
Andreea Michaud	US	klangwelt.com
Maximilian Mauracher	AT	maximilianmauracher.com
Natalie Zart	AT	nataliezart.com
Wolfgang Hartl	AT	amstein.at
Julia Weithaler	AT	dschuleia.com
Andreas Aust	AT	aa-newperspective.com

The finalization of this book was also supported by Anthony "Naz" Iannazzi, Anna Uidl, Annique Senten, Ani Bagdasaryan, Benjamin White, Bastian Eggers, Daniela Wiebogen, Ekaterina Hazard, Heather Corcoran, Harald Eckmüller, Jonathon Dyer, Jennifer Maire Brown, Karin Zölzer, Malia Gonzales, Matthew Strother, Matt Alcock, Melanie Samec, Martina Nadvornikova, Paul Koerber, Robert Ojamo, Rosemarie Reiter, Sarah Marie Roberts, Steve Finan, Tummarong Ingpongpun, and 196 other #SMARTCREATIVES! Thank you!

THANK YOU TO OUR REVIEWERS

We're grateful Work Trips and Road Trips was reviewed by people we admire greatly, so we'd love for you to check out their work:

Annie Daly is always at the right place at the right time. She has a CV you won't even believe is real. She's a brand editor at *Self Magazine*, but her work's also been published on BuzzFeed, Time Out New York, *Elle* ... I could keep name-dropping. She has her own, super catchy, and unique way with words, which is why we asked her to tell us what she thinks about WTART!

Emma Gannon is a real power woman. Her book, *CTRL ALT DELETE: How I Grew Up Online*, tells the story of the millennial generation and what it was like growing up with the social web at your finger tips. Emma loves to gather creative people either online for her podcast, or at one of her events in London. If you're in the city, make it your business to show up! You won't regret!

Kathi Kamleitner is a travel blogger and a film journalist. She's a courageous free spirit who loves nothing more than to inspire people to explore the world. As a regular contributor to the Travelettes, she shows women that they can dare to travel solo too! Her enthusiasm and passion is catchy and it's hard to not feel uplifted when you read something she wrote or listen to something she said!

Katy Cowan is the mastermind behind the *Creative Boom*, an online art and design magazine that always surprises you with creative work you haven't seen everywhere else! She's also the founder of the Manchester-based PR agency, Boomerang. Katy's kindness and love for the things she does are incredibly admirable!

GET MY OTHER BOOKS

Thank you for reading *Work Trips and Road Trips* to the very end!
If you'd love to get some more inspiration you can buy *This Year Will Be Different: The insightful guide to becoming a freelancer* and also *My Creative (Side) Business: The insightful guide to turning your side projects into a full-time creative business* on Amazon.
If you'd love to get notified about my upcoming publications, sign up for bit.ly/newpublications

Write a review and get a present: if you want to share your love, please write us an Amazon review, send us a screenshot and your postal address to hello@mkanokova.com and we'll send you some beautifully illustrated cards as a thank you!